It's not complicated: if
it. And *Long Story Short*
book is a brilliant overview of the whole Bible story,
covering the major plot points without getting lost in
the weeds. Ideal for non-believers and new believers,
Glen's knack for avoiding insider jargon shines.
Filled with fresh insight and vivid prose, there were
moments I forgot I had encountered this epic story
before.

MATT SMETHURST
Managing Editor, The Gospel Coalition,
Author of *1–2 Thessalonians: A 12-Week Study*

The greatest story ever told is typically ignored. After
all, most people are not too excited about wading into
a big dusty Bible. In Long Story Short, Glen deftly
leads us through the great story in twelve decisive
steps. Enjoy these twelve stepping stones and you are
going to want to blow the dust off your Bible. More
than that, you are going to be surprised how much
you want to get to know the hero of the story himself!

PETER MEAD
Director of Cor Deo,
Leader of Bible Teachers & Preachers Network at the
European Leadership Forum,
Author of several books, including *Pleased to Dwell*

Classic Scrivener. Simple without being simplistic,
smart without being smug, bubbling over with ideas
but never losing sight of the person at the centre of it
all. Glen doesn't assume you think any of this stuff

is true, but be warned: he has a gift for making you wish it were.

BARRY COOPER
Author and Co-Founder of Christianity Explored Ministries

The gospel is a powerful drama of a great fall and a heroic rise. Glen Scrivener adds color and context to the beautiful story of redemption found in the Bible. This book will contribute to your love for all that was accomplished through the living, dying, and rising of Jesus of Nazareth.

DAN DEWITT
Author of *Life in the Wild*,
Associate Professor of Applied Theology and Apologetics,
Cedarville University, Ohio

If you are one of those people who is prepared to sit down and give a bit of time to understanding someone else's perspective, then when it comes to getting a handle on the Christian story, this is just a great place to start. Glen Scrivener — the Australian Oxford-educated stand-up comedian — is a unique communicator and here wonderfully he brings his profound gifts to bear, as he tells what Christians believe is the greatest story ever told. But be warned, I really don't think you can read this glorious helicopter ride over the Bible story and remain unchanged!

RICO TICE
Author, Christianity Explored & Associate Minister at All Souls Church, Langham Place, London

What a feast! This is a fresh, engaging and thought provoking retelling of God's story. There's lots of insight into Bible truths combined with timely application to our contemporary lives. By taking in the whole sweep of bible narrative Glen's book brings into view and connects together parts of the story arc that can easy get missed. This Bible overview will renew your delight that God's wondrous story is your story and is good for the soul.

ANDREW BAUGHEN
Director of Soulful Enterprise,
Author of *The Because Approach*

# LONG

# STORY

# SHORT

## THE BIBLE IN 12 PHRASES

### GLEN SCRIVENER

**CHRISTIAN**
**FOCUS**

Copyright © Glen Scrivener 2018

paperback ISBN 978-1-5271-0176-0

epub ISBN 978-1-5271-0245-3

mobi ISBN 978-1-5271-0246-0

First published in 2018
by
Christian Focus Publications Ltd,
Geanies House, Fearn, Ross-shire,
IV20 1TW, Scotland
www.christianfocus.com

A CIP catalogue record for this book is available from
the British Library

Printed and bound by Bell & Bain, Glasgow

MIX
Paper from
responsible sources
FSC
www.fsc.org      FSC® C007785

Cover design by Daniel Van Straaten
Internal illustrations by Jason Ramasami (www.saamvisual.com)

# CONTENTS

Introduction: Long Story........................ 11

1.  In the Beginning ...................... 17

2.  As Old as Adam ....................... 29

3.  God Will Provide...................... 41

4.  Burning Bush ......................... 53

5.  Thou Shalt............................ 63

6.  Scapegoat ............................ 75

7.  Land of Milk and Honey ............... 85

*Catch Up 1: From Creation to Kings* ........... 97

8.  Giant Killing.......................... 99

*Catch Up 2: Words of the Wise* ............... 109

9.  Getting Carried Away ................. 113

*Catch Up 3: The Prophets and the Return*...... 125

10. The Heavens Opened ................. 127

11. Damascus Road ...................... 139

12. Hallelujah ........................... 153

Epilogue: And You?........................... 163

*For Ruby*
*The apple of my eye*

# INTRODUCTION:
# LONG STORY

The Bible is a big book—in more ways than one.

To start with, it's more like a library than a paperback: sixty-six mini-books written over 1500 years by forty authors from three continents.

This can be a little daunting—especially for first-time readers. You may have all kinds of questions: Where do I begin? How do I understand it? What's the big idea? I hope this book will help with that.

But it's not just the Bible's size that's big: its impact is too. Socially, morally, artistically, politically, even scientifically, it has 'turned the world upside down' (to use one of its phrases). In fact, we can't understand our world, until we understand this book.

One of the simplest ways to see its impact is through language. The Bible has shaped the English we speak more than any other source. At some point this week, if not today, you're likely to quote the Bible, even if you 'know not what you do'!

It's given us hundreds of phrases: 'No rest for the wicked', 'Labour of love', 'Wits' end', 'The powers that be', 'God forbid', 'The apple of my eye', 'Money's the root of all evil', 'Atonement', 'By the skin of my teeth', 'Fly in the ointment', 'Once and for all'. We may not know their source or even their meaning, but the Bible is forever 'putting words in our mouth'.

I've written this book to answer two questions about the Bible: the *what* and the *why*. What is the Bible about and why has it changed the world? These are huge questions—but they have one answer. There's one story that runs through this book, explaining not only the Bible but *everything else*: from life and death, to hope and humanity.

How is this possible? Because the Bible's long story is actually a biography. It's not about ideas, it's about a person. As we meet *him*, everything else starts to make sense.

Jesus is both the heart of the Bible and the secret of its power. He illuminates the Scriptures, but he also sheds light on our lives. That's why he is described as 'the Light of the world'.

## SEEING THE LIGHT

Let me say straight away: I don't presume that you believe in the Bible or in Jesus. I am assuming no prior Christian knowledge or experience. But I hope that as you explore the Bible you will start to see things differently. How might that happen?

Well, think of that *other* light of the world—the sun. We can appreciate the sun in two ways. We can look at it in all its glory and be wowed by its brilliance. But we can also look at *everything else* in the light of the sun. Both kinds of looking will help us appreciate the sun. It's the same with Jesus.

I hope that you will explore the Bible as you read these short chapters. Try on these biblical phrases and stories like glasses and look around. My prayer is that you will see the dazzling beauty of Jesus—that's the whole reason the Bible was written. I also hope that you will look at the world around you and see how it's illuminated by the truth and love of Jesus. I trust that, with Jesus at the centre, you'll start to make sense of more than just the Bible. You'll make sense of life.

That's what happened to me many years ago. I was unemployed with plenty of time on my hands. I'm not entirely sure why, but I picked up a Bible and began to read of Jesus. At some point—I couldn't tell you when—I 'saw the Light'. It occurred to me that Jesus was The One. He's what life is all about.

As I met this Person who was full of love and compassion, I began to make sense of my world. I'd always thought that 'love was the greatest thing'. I'd always assumed that personal relationships, truth, beauty, goodness and compassion were the stuff of real life. But, more and more, those things began to make sense as illuminated by *his* radiance. Jesus seemed both to *be* a dazzling Light *and* to enlighten the world around me. And so I found myself 'believing'. No-one *told* me to believe in Jesus. It just dawned on me that Jesus was *it*.

The Bible has a phrase to describe what a Christian is. A Christian is someone who knows that 'Jesus is Lord'. In other words, we think he's ultimate, the best, tops, *numero uno*. No-one has to convince me that the sun is bright—I see it and I know. And no-one has to convince me that Jesus is Lord—I see him in the Bible and I know.

My prayer is that you will try on the Bible like a pair of glasses and 'see the Light'. When you do—everything changes.

## WHAT'S AHEAD?

This book is structured around twelve famous phrases from the Bible. There are nine from the Old Testament—that's the part written 'BC', before Christ came as a man. There are three from the New Testament—the part written 'AD', after Christ came in the flesh. We go from the first book (Genesis), to the last book (Revelation) and we'll sketch out the Bible's story along the way.

At points you'll spot a 'catch up' section that fills in some of the gaps of the Bible's timeline. Use these if they're helpful—but feel free to skip them too.

This is just a taste of the Bible's feast—if you're still hungry, there's plenty more! Further reading is suggested at the end of each chapter, as well as some questions for further reflection. Why not chat them through with a friend?

Finally, a technical point: I'll often refer to Bible verses like Genesis 49:10. That means it's the *book* of Genesis, *chapter* 49 and *verse* 10. The chapters are marked in your Bible by the large numbers, the verses are marked by the little ones. I recommend having a Bible to hand so you can look up the passages and chase up the references.

Are you sitting comfortably? Then we'll begin.

# 1
# In the Beginning

Opening lines can be hard to write. But some have captured our imaginations:

Now is the winter of our discontent... — *Richard III.*

It was the best of times, it was the worst of times. — *A Tale of Two Cities*

A long time ago in a galaxy far, far away... — *Star Wars*

High, high above the North Pole, on the first day of 1969, two professors of English Literature approached each other at a combined velocity of 1200 miles per hour. — *Changing Places*, by David Lodge

With a good opening line, the author grabs us and draws us into their world. This is what the Bible does in its very first verse:

> In the beginning God created the heavens and the earth. (Gen. 1:1)

We're being told: here is an epic tale. Here is a sweeping drama that encompasses all time—right back to 'the beginning'. It also takes in all space—the heavens and the earth. And as for its central character—well, nothing less than God himself! The Bible's 'beginning' could not be bigger.

We've heard the Bible's verdict, but what do *you* believe about 'the beginning'? It's a vital issue, but one we rarely consider. So let's try a little thought experiment: what do *you* say was there 'in the beginning'? I realise it's odd to think like this, but give it a go. In your mind see if you can wind back the cosmic clock into the depths of forever.

When I've asked people to do this they commonly respond with: 'cave men, dinosaurs, planets, the sun, galaxies'. I have to say, 'No, keep going. *Before* those. What was there... before people or planets or protons?' At that point we're dealing with *ultimate* reality. 'In the beginning' we figure out what we really believe. Are you there? What's it like? What is ultimate reality for you?

I think there are four main ways of conceiving of 'the beginning'. These four approaches are not mutually exclusive—there's much overlap between them—but our thinking in this area will shape everything we believe about ourselves, our world and our destiny.

Let's start with the first: What was there in the beginning?

## NOTHING

'In the beginning' there was... nothing. A big, dark, endless expanse of empty space (of course, that's not nothing, that's a whole lot of black *something*, but let's not get picky).

I don't know about you, but this is my first thought:

*Before* the universe? But the universe is everything! What could possibly come before it?!

That's probably my first thought because this is the story I've grown up with in the West. In this story our origins lie in some absolute zero point. Bring it all back to basics and what do you get? Nothing. Shakespeare's King Lear said 'Nothing will come of nothing.' But this story says that everything comes from nothing. We have sprung from nothing, are suspended over nothing and are headed for nothing. Right now we enjoy a brief moment in the sun but as Lawrence Krauss, the author of the book *A Universe From Nothing*, is always reminding us:

The two lessons I want to give people is that you're more insignificant than you ever thought, and the future is miserable.[1]

---

1. *Why a Universe From Nothing Should Mean Everything*, from The Huffington Post, 20 July, 2012, http://www.huffington-post.com/rebecca-searles/universe-origins_b_1687559.html

Well, at least he's honest. If we've come from nothing there are implications! What does life *mean* in the 'nothing' story? It means trying to work a something out of a nothing. Make your own reason for being, construct your own image, be a self-creator. There's just one problem: in the end, we go back to basics. Less than basics. We finish how we began—with nothing.

The artist Damien Hirst is brilliant at portraying life from within this mind-set. His artwork includes dead animals preserved in formaldehyde, neon coffins and diamond encrusted skulls. The glitz on the surface might dazzle, but beneath there is only death—only annihilation.

When asked about the motivation behind his art, Hirst at one point responded, 'it's like everything you do in life is pointless if you just take a step back and look at it'.[2] That sounds horribly bleak. But Hirst is just giving us a little perspective. If there was Nothing in the beginning, he's absolutely right.

Life in its brevity can be beautiful. In close-up there are diamonds to behold, but push beneath and there's nothing. We find we're suspended over a void and soon we will fall into it.

Beliefs about 'the beginning' matter. If there was nothing, then life is *ultimately* absurd.

---

2. Damien Hirst: 'We're here for a good time, not a long time', The Telegraph, 8 January, 2011. http://www.telegraph.co.uk/culture/art/art-features/8245906/Damien-Hirst-Were-here-for-a-good-time-not-a-long-time.html

So what are the alternatives? Let's think about the second option. What was there in the beginning?

## CHAOS

The Genesis account of creation is remarkable when you compare it with the religious texts of its time and place. In Genesis 1 we read of a good world spoken into existence by a good God. Seas, lands and sky are formed at God's word—everything in its right place and filled with light and life (see verses 3-31).

By way of immense contrast the prominent creation myths of antiquity tell of wars in heaven. Battling gods jostle for pre-eminence and the losers are cast out. Perhaps creation is the place of exile for naughty deities or the body of a dead god. Or maybe the universe is just the rubble of some cosmic storm. However these spiritual battles are imagined, life springs from the collision of raging forces.

Of course it's not just religious stories that speak of the force of chaos. Science too tells us we have come from a big *bang*, the collision of stars and the struggle for survival. So much of life *is* about conflict, killing and chaos. That cannot be denied. But there are some who say that this is *ultimately* what shapes reality. Trace it all back to basics and you'll find no guiding hand, no rhyme nor reason, no law higher than 'the law of the jungle'. If this were true, then, essentially, life would be a struggle with no 'Geneva Convention' to appeal to.

Few people can stomach the chaos story. Surely there must be some governing principles that rule over the turmoil? That brings many people to a third option. What was there in the beginning?

## POWER

Again, there's a religious and a non-religious version of this one. The non-religious version says this: 'In the beginning there were colossal forces.' Reality is ruled by iron laws of physics that grind along. The universe dances to this relentless beat.

On 2 September 2010 the front page of The Times declared: 'God did not create the universe'. What a scoop! Their source was a book co-authored by Stephen Hawking. He said:

> Because there is a law such as gravity, the universe can and will create itself from nothing.

There are a number of puzzles we won't try to solve here. Puzzles like:

- *Is this really 'nothing'?* Laws of nature seem like some pretty significant somethings.

- *How does anything 'create itself'?* Doesn't it have to exist already if it's going to do any creating?

- *How do laws 'create'?* The rules of chess don't create the pieces, how do the laws of nature create nature?

We will jump over those objections and try to follow Hawking. Imagine that 'a law such as gravity' does indeed lie behind everything. Let's inhabit the story in which there is nothing higher, older or deeper than laws of nature. These cosmic powers are the un-moulded moulders of everything else and we dance to their relentless beat. Power reigns.

Many people find this to be a particularly barren account of reality. In a world of love, laughter and lemon drizzle cake, gravity and the laws of thermodynamics seem an unsatisfying explanation. No-one denies that natural forces play their part. But are such impersonal powers supreme? Is there nothing beneath or beyond them?

Maybe we should abandon that kind of atheism and run, shrieking, into the arms of religion. Is that a solution to this bleak view of the world? No. I don't think so. Religion is no kind of answer to this problem. All too often, religion is just another version of the 'power' story.

When you ask a generally religious person to describe 'the beginning', they might well mention God. But ask them 'Which God?' and you get some worrying answers. Often the description of God 'in the beginning' sounds like this: 'He was bored'. 'He was lonely.' 'He was contemplating himself.' 'He was planning creation.' Almost everyone thinks of God as a solitary individual. Even Christians, who should know better. But actually, such a thought is chilling.

Can you imagine this solitary god existing from all eternity? He has no-one and nothing beside him, just his own thoughts for company. This god knows nothing of relationship, nothing of back-and-forth or give-and-take. This god is not *essentially* loving. This god is simply 'power' by another name.

If this god were really God, how must his creatures relate to him? We must submit to his absolute will. We cannot trust the love of this god; we can only fear his power.

If this god was 'in the beginning', then we'd be saved from nothingness, we'd be saved from chaos… but we'd be delivered into slavery.

Is this what the Bible means when it starts 'In the beginning God'? Wonderfully, no. That's not the God of the Bible at all.

Here is the Bible's answer to our question. What was there in the beginning?

## LOVE

This is an answer that changes everything. If it is true, it is the greatest of all truths—the Bible insists that we've come from love, we're shaped by love. Love rules our lives, our world and our future.

Could that be true? The Bible says, Think back to 'the beginning'. There you'll see that ultimate reality is not a lonely individual but a lively interplay. Let me explain.

The phrase 'in the beginning' appears three times in the Bible. Once at the start of Genesis and then twice at the start of John in the New Testament.

Genesis says that, 'In the beginning God created the heavens and the earth'. It goes on to describe God's creation in *plural* terms. The Spirit of God moves upon the waters (Gen. 1:2). The Word of God brings everything into being (v.3). God has a Word and a Spirit and does all things through his Word and by his Spirit.

In the New Testament, John begins his Gospel by writing: 'In the beginning was the Word, and the Word was with God, and the Word was God. He was with God in the beginning' (John 1:1-2).

Here John is refreshing our memory of Genesis. In the beginning there was not a lonely god. In the beginning there was one Person called 'God', later called 'the Father' (v. 14). Then there was a second Person called 'the Word'. He can also take the name 'God' (v. 1), 'the Son of God' (v. 14, NIV 2011) and 'Jesus Christ' (v. 17). Finally, John introduces us to a third Person—the 'Holy Spirit' or 'Comforter'.[3] He too is 'God'. He too was there 'in the beginning'.

According to the Bible, this is what was there 'in the beginning'—the Father, Son and Holy Spirit. Ultimate reality is a loving union of Three. Christians call this 'the Trinity', which is just a way of squashing two words together: *tri* and *unity*. The Triunity (or Trinity) is the unbreakable and eternal unity of these Three. *That's* who God is, and who he has always been.

And here's what it means. For all eternity there *was* give-and-take, back-and-forth. There was friendliness. Therefore God is not defined by supremacy but by sharing.

---

3. e.g. John 16:5-16 (KJV).

In short, as a famous verse says, 'God is love' (1 John 4:8). Essentially—right down to his bootstraps you might say—the Father has been loving his Son in the joy of the Spirit. This love is not just what the Three do, it's who they are. Their love is too good to keep to themselves. The Father, Son and Spirit want to share.

*This* is the reason for creation. The God of love overflows like a fountain brimming with life. He reaches out, to draw billions more into this love.

## WELCOMED BY THE GOD OF LOVE

I was the youngest child in my family by some distance. My parents called me a 'surprise'; my sisters 'a mistake'. Strangely, I didn't like being called 'a mistake'. I liked to think of myself as carefully planned, eagerly anticipated and utterly wanted. We all do.

The Bible tells us that we're not a mistake or even just a pleasant surprise. We are wanted. We are the planned offspring of the God of love and he longs to share his life with us.

## WHAT DO YOU THINK?

We have begun with some mind-expanding concepts. Really that's inescapable. The Bible's 'beginning' forces us to think big. I wonder how you react?

Whatever beliefs we hold, all of us should admit that there is much that is true about the nothing, chaos and power stories. This world *is* full of impersonal powers, chaotic forces and the threat of nothingness. Even if we believe that 'God is love' we must all confess that not everything is lovely. Far from it. In the next chapter we will consider how those darker realities have come to mar God's good world. But here's the question for this chapter: Are those forces *ultimate*? Is life *fundamentally* about Nothingness? Chaos? Power? Or is there a reality that runs even deeper?

Maybe you think we've come from *nothing*? If so our lives are, ultimately, absurd.

Perhaps we have emerged from *chaos*? Then it's all just a struggle.

Is everything simply about *power*? In which case we're determined by forces that enslave us.

The Bible says that these things are not *ultimate*. There was something else 'in the beginning'. If you put your finger on the pulse of reality, you'll find the God of **love**. And through Jesus, we're invited in.

*Keep reading…*

Genesis 1:1–2:3
John 1:1-18
Colossians 1:15-20

*Keep thinking…*

As you consider what was 'in the beginning', which answer(s) best describe your beliefs? Are there any answers not listed here?

Do you see the link between 'In the beginning', our present life now, and our future? What is it?

Have you considered 'the Trinity' before? How would it change your view of God, of the world, and of life's meaning?

# 2

# As Old as Adam

The Bible's 'beginning' holds out a dazzling poss-
ibility. What if love is ultimate? What if before and
beneath, above and beyond this world *love* reigns
supreme? It's a breath-taking thought.

But we shouldn't get too carried away. Not yet. The
Bible is anything but utopian. Almost as soon as we're
presented with this heavenly reality, Genesis brings
us crashing down to earth again. By the time we get
to page 3 we read the Adam story and everything
descends from paradise to the pit. Things fall apart.
And you think 'typical'. Well, yes. Exactly. That's
how we're meant to respond to Adam: 'Typical!' He's
typical of everything that's wrong with the world.

In the Bible, Adam is an original and universal
figure. He's Everyman. As we read his story we're
meant to see ourselves represented. Two modern
sayings about Adam capture this truth. The first is...

## 'AS OLD AS ADAM'

If something is ancient, it's said to be 'as old as Adam'. The phrase often alludes to a stubborn fact of existence that won't be changed.

Frustrations with work, the battle of the sexes, in-growing toenails—'as old as Adam'. This troublesome feature of life is nothing new—nothing to be surprised about. Here is a state of affairs you can't get around. Broken relationships, shattered dreams, depression, disease, death—these are 'as old as Adam'.

As we consider this, there should be a deep sense of sadness and even helplessness. We seem incapable of escaping this ancient legacy. And perhaps as we label our problems in this way there's an overtone of blame being laid on Adam. Biblically speaking, that's appropriate. He is the ultimate fall-guy, as we'll see.

Let's consider another saying...

## 'HE DOESN'T KNOW ME FROM ADAM'

This phrase means 'he doesn't know me at all'. You could say 'he doesn't know me from a sack of potatoes'. It's interesting, though, that *Adam* is the one we'd like to be distinguished from. A stranger needs to know my difference from Adam. Right now I might as well *be* Adam to this person.

I find that fascinating. Biblically speaking, there's a deep sense in which you *won't* know me from Adam. I'm the same as you and we're the same as everyone else. 'We are family', as the old song says.

One of the disturbing aspects of growing up is realising how much you are shaped by your family.

Perhaps you find yourself dispensing home-spun morals to a friend and as the words leave your mouth, you despair: 'I'm becoming my mother!' Or you make a lame joke to the waitress and, please no, *Dad humour* has overtaken you. It springs forth, unbidden, from primeval fountains and there's nothing we can do. We are our families, and this applies globally. The Bible says that we share 'family traits' because we are in fact family. And these traits are 'fallen' traits.

## FALL FROM GRACE

We often speak of 'the fall' in daily conversation. Perhaps we speak of a 'fall from grace' (Gal. 5:4) or lament 'How the mighty have fallen' (2 Sam. 1:19) or we quote the old Proverb: 'Pride goes before a fall' (based on Prov. 16:18).

With all these sayings we're used to pointing the finger. We like to see 'tall poppies' cut down to size! But the Bible has an uncomfortable truth for us. It says that *we* have fallen from grace. All of us. And it's our pride that has tripped us up.

Certainly we began on high. In Genesis 2 Adam was given a 'match made in heaven' to be his 'other half'. Eve was famously taken from Adam's side, something that, besides anything else, communicates her equality. As the seventeenth century preacher, Matthew Henry put it:

> Woman was... not made out of [Adam's] head to rule over him, nor out of his feet to be trampled upon by him, but out of his side to be equal with him, under

31

his arm to be protected, and near his heart to be beloved.[1]

If Adam was dust, Eve was dust twice refined. If Adam was head over creation, Eve was the crown. When they were brought together, Adam bursts into the world's first love song: 'This at last is bone of my bones and flesh of my flesh' (Gen. 2:23, ESV).

This was the 'grace' and 'might' from which we fell, as pride ruined it all.

## INTO TEMPTATION

Genesis chapter 3 is a famous scene depicted in art, literature and film. For that reason it can be hard to take seriously. But it's important to get a proper understanding.

The chapter opens with the entrance of a wise and powerful creature: 'the serpent'. But we're not meant to picture 'a talking snake'. The Bible insists that he's an angelic creature. He was there to guard the couple.[2] He was not placed in the garden as an evil power but a benevolent one. He fell, just as the humans did. And, as with the humans, it was pride that was his downfall.

In Genesis 3 we do not see a capricious God putting humanity in harm's way. No, this is about conniving creatures—human and angelic—allying themselves

---

1. *Matthew Henry's Commentary on the Whole Bible: Complete and unabridged*, Matthew Henry, Hendrickson Publishers Marketing, LLC, 1990, comment on Genesis 2:21-25.

2. Ezekiel 28:12-17.

against their Creator. Through this ancient story we see humanity and the serpent goading each other on towards the brink. In the end they jump, hand in hand. And it all began with mistrust.

The serpent says to Eve:

> Did God really say, 'You must not eat from any tree in the garden'? (Gen. 3:1)

God in fact did *not* forbid eating from 'any tree in the garden'. God is not a selfish giant, walling off his garden from pesky fruit-pickers. He's a generous Lord who plants a garden *for* his beloved children. In Genesis 2, God had said, 'You are free to eat from any tree in the garden' (Gen. 2:16). This garden was a place of almost unimaginable freedom. There was only one restriction, just one forbidden fruit (Gen. 2:17).

Why this one boundary? Well, consider the alternative. If there was literally nothing humanity could do to demonstrate *mistrust* of God, then there would also be nothing they could do to demonstrate their *trust* of God. So with this tree there is one opportunity to express their allegiance to God. It was very simple. They didn't have to go on a long pilgrimage or perform a list of tasks. They simply had to refrain from doing one thing. But even that one thing proved too much.

Eve says to the serpent:

> We may eat fruit from the trees in the garden, but God did say, 'You must not eat fruit from the tree

that is in the middle of the garden, and you must not touch it, or you will die'.

This is the first actual lie. In his opening gambit, the serpent hadn't said anything wrong, not technically. The very first misstep in history was a human one, and it consisted in the addition of a rule. It was not God who multiplied laws in the garden; humanity did that. The first sin was to add to God's requirements. And without missing a beat the serpent piles on with an out-and-out lie:

'You will not surely die,' the serpent said to the woman. 'For God knows that when you eat from it your eyes will be opened, and you will be like God'. (Gen. 3:5)

In this back-and-forth we've gone from doubting God to doubling his laws and now denying his word. All of it springs from a suspicion of God's character. As we read it feels so familiar. It's meant to. The Bible says we all mistrust our Maker. Deep down we doubt his goodness and question his guidance. Just the phrase 'forbidden fruit' makes our mouths water. That tells you everything you need to know about the human nature we've inherited from Adam. We basically doubt that God is for us, so we think that real life will be found by turning elsewhere.

This is the problem that's 'as old as Adam'—mutinous mistrust. What this couple did, we always do. We too turn from the goodness of God, trust our own judgement and pursue life on our own terms.

And it must mean a catastrophic fall. How could it not?

If God is the source of life, then rejecting him must mean death. If he is light, then turning away must mean darkness. If God is love then refusing him must leave us disconnected—from him and from each other.

That is how the story unfolds in Genesis 3. Adam and Eve choose against life, light and love and therefore are plunged into death, darkness and disconnection. That's their story, and it's our story too.

## UNIVERSAL ADDICTION

Many people have wondered to themselves: 'Would I have acted in the garden the way that Adam did?' But that's not really the way to think about it. According to the Bible, we simply find ourselves in this dysfunctional family called the human race. Our negative family traits—like mistrust, disobedience and pride—simply prove that Adam's sin is original to us all.

Recently I spoke to a recovering heroin addict. He told me he was interested in Christianity but this teaching about Adam was a real turn off. 'I could never believe in "original sin"', he said. 'Original sin' is one name for what we're talking about here. It's the doctrine, taught in the Bible,[3] that sees Adam's story as our story. 'Original sin' says we're not atomistic individuals with a neutral moral character. Actually

---

3. e.g. Romans 5:12.

we're part of a global human family and a global human problem. According to 'original sin' we are born into ancient and universal family traits like selfishness, deception and greed. My friend didn't like that teaching. But, intriguingly, within ninety seconds of expressing his dislike for 'original sin' he said, 'I've got a theory of my own: I reckon we're all addicts. *All* of us.'

I liked this 'new' theory of his. We decided to give it a name: 'universal addiction'. We set about formulating the doctrine of 'universal addiction', it went something like this:

> Everyone is ruled by desires. These desires get twisted and end up destroying us and those around us. We get overwhelmed by desires for the wrong things. Or we want the right things for the wrong reasons or in the wrong proportions. Some people are addicted to heroin, some to praise, some to comfort, some to power, some to sex, some to work, some to money, but everyone's addicted.

It was an excellent theory—demonstrably true and with immense explanatory power. But of course it's really the Bible's teaching by another name. Whatever we call it—'original sin', 'universal addiction'—it doesn't matter, the truth remains that humans are stuck. Through the Adam story, the Bible is telling us what we already know: the human condition involves profound brokenness and frustration. And no-one is exempt.

The next time you say something deceitful, hurtful or proud, you cannot say 'I don't know what came over me.' Nothing came over you. Such sins come *out* of you. They come from a well-spring that is very dark, very deep and very old. You know it. We all feel it. Adam explains it.

## REJECTING MYTHS

At this point the Adam story is on a collision course with our modern origins story. These days, in the West, we tend to see people as blank slates as they come into the world. We reckon we are individuals who are born good (or at least neutral) and infinite possibilities lie ahead for us. We can make of ourselves whatever we choose. That's the western dogma anyway.

As origins stories go, this modern one is the truly mythological one. It runs counter to everything we know in the sociological, psychological and neuro-scientific realms. No-one is a blank slate. We all come into the world with a thousand pre-conditions both external and internal. We don't choose our genetic make-up; we don't choose the century we're born in, the culture, the race, the gender, the family. We don't choose our upbringing, our education, our formative experiences. In short we have absolutely no say over that which constitutes the vast majority of 'our personal identity'. Yet still the myth persists that we are born as neutral, decision-making individuals. We like to imagine ourselves as self-made men and women whose choices, hard work and ingenuity determine our lives. But such thinking is magical.

By contrast, Genesis tells a far more prosaic origins story. It tells us what we should already know: we are the product of our families.

According to the Bible, the issue is not *whether* we are determined by our family. The question is *which* family will determine us.

## WHICH FAMILY?

Amidst all this talk of our families determining us there is a glimmer of hope in Genesis. From the beginning the Bible actually holds out another 'family' to belong to—a good one. We studied this 'family' in the last chapter. I put 'family' in quotes because the analogy only goes so far, but in chapter 1 we encountered a Father who loves his Son in the joy of the Holy Spirit. *This* 'family', if I'm allowed to use such language, is where we truly belong. This 'family' is God's own life of loving unity. And in Genesis 3 we are told that there is a bridge from that perfect family into our dysfunctional family. The Son of God would become our Brother.

Even as the whole world is falling apart, a promise is spoken. In verse 15, the Lord God says to the serpent:

> I will put enmity
>     between you and the woman,
> and between your offspring and hers;
>     he will crush your head,
> and you will strike his heel.

These are enigmatic words but they speak of a man who will come. He's called 'the offspring', or you could say 'the seed'. It's the same word in Hebrew (the language in which the Old Testament was written). Later generations would call him 'the Messiah' (which in Greek, the language of the New Testament, is 'Christ'). This is the hope: the Son of God would be born into the world as a human offspring. He would join our family to put right what we had done wrong. He would conquer Satan in a fight to the death—though he would be struck, he would gain the victory.

Even as everything was falling apart, Genesis was preaching the good news about Jesus. The hope is held out that one day the Son would be a second Adam, born to answer the first.[4] Where Adam proudly grasped at life, Christ would humbly give his life. Where Adam fell for Satan's lies, Christ would conquer. And this second Adam would give us a second family to belong to—God's.

The New Testament puts it like this: 'Everyone dies because all of us are related to Adam... But all who are related to Christ will rise again' (1 Cor. 15:22, TLB). We are all shaped by our family; this is an inescapable truth. But we don't have to be determined by Adam's dysfunctional family. There is another 'family' to belong to. The story of the Bible is the story of Christ, the Son of God, joining us in our brokenness to bring us home.

---

4. 1 Corinthians 15:45.

*Keep reading...*

> Genesis 2:4-25
> Genesis 3:1-24
> Romans 5:12-21

*Keep thinking...*

How has your family and your family history shaped your identity?

Can you see how Adam's actions have changed things for us? How do you feel about this?

In what ways are Adam and Christ similar? In what ways are they different?

# 3

# God Will Provide

What *is* the Bible?

Sometimes Christians are the worst at answering that question. Some will reply: 'The Maker's Instruction Manual'. Or 'God's Road Map'. Creative types have given us an acronym: BIBLE apparently stands for 'Basic Instructions Before Leaving Earth'. Most often, people, whether Christians or not, see it as essentially a moral guidebook.

If ever there was a story to explode that myth, though, it's Genesis chapter 22. This is the place where Abraham has his infamous test of faith. Indeed the story has tested more than Abraham's faith. It has proved a stumbling block for many. How can a holy book speak of, well, *child sacrifice*!? What's going on?

Before we study it, we need to catch ourselves up on the story so far.

## EAST OF EDEN

After Adam and Eve are kicked out of paradise, the human family gets going 'east of Eden'. Straight away there's trouble (see Gen. 4:1-16). The very first offspring of Eve is born and there might have been high hopes; after all, the promise was that the Offspring would be born of woman and save the world! Unfortunately Eve's first offspring was not the Messiah. He was—and I really can't resist saying this, so forgive me—a *very* naughty boy. Cain was not a Saviour but a slayer, killing his brother Abel and then becoming 'a restless wanderer on the earth' (v.14). He too travels east (v.16). This seems to be the direction of estrangement from God.

In Genesis 5 we find a genealogy that pounds into us a relentless drumbeat of death.

> *So and so* lived *so many years* and had *such and such children* **and then he died**.

The cycle is repeated generation after generation. 'And then he died... And then he died... And then he died.' The glory of Eden is all but forgotten and the decline is not just physical. It's spiritual. By the time we get to Genesis 6 the Lord's verdict on humanity could not be more bleak:

> The LORD saw how great the wickedness of the human race had become on the earth, and that every inclination of the thoughts of the human heart was only evil all the time. The LORD regretted that he had made human beings on the earth, and his heart

was deeply troubled. So the LORD said, 'I will wipe from the face of the earth the human race I have created—and with them the animals, the birds and the creatures that move along the ground—for I regret that I have made them.' (Gen. 6:5-7, NIV 2011)

In Genesis 6–9 we read about this cataclysmic judgement—the flood. In the story, one man, Noah, finds favour in God's eyes and is counted righteous. This righteous man (and his ark) becomes the safe place for all who would hide in him. When judgement strikes, those who trust the LORD gather to the righteous one to find safe passage through the storms and on the far side of judgement there is a new world. Even the animals are included.

The Bible is clear that this event is a picture of the judgement and salvation that Jesus will bring (cf. Matt. 24:37-39; 1 Pet. 3:20-22; 2 Pet. 3:3-7). He is the truly righteous one to whom we gather, and those hidden in him will come through to a world that is truly renewed. That is the future; but in Genesis, though the world was deluged, it was not cleansed. Not decisively. Wickedness re-emerges, even before the Noah story has concluded (Gen. 9:18-29), and humanity keeps heading east (Gen. 11:2).

In Genesis 11 the people devise a plan:

Come, let us build ourselves a city, with a tower that reaches to the heavens, so that we may make a name for ourselves and not be scattered over the face of the whole earth. (Gen. 11:4)

God's first promise was for the man of heaven to descend and save us. Humanity's plan is to ascend to heaven and 'make a name for ourselves'. God and humanity are on a collision course and in Genesis 11 God scatters everything. He scatters this 'tower of Babel'; he scatters the peoples, their language, their common understanding. His way is not the way of building upwards. He is the God who comes down, and the next story—the story of Abraham—will present that lesson over and over again.

## REVERSING THE ROT

By the time we meet Abraham we are at our most easterly point. He's living in Ur of the Chaldees (modern day Iraq). It's around 2000 BC and it seems like God has had enough of our easterly drift. He plucks Abraham out of his old life and calls him back west, to the promised land (the land of Canaan). God is starting something new: not an eastward, upward people, but a westward, downward people.

In Genesis chapter 12, Abraham is told that God will 'make a name' for Abraham. This is the opposite of the tower of Babel. Instead of humanity lifting itself up, God's blessing comes down (Gen. 12:1-3). Abraham is established as the head of a family that will bless the world. All this comes through the promise of 'offspring'. Through Abraham's offspring the way of Babel will be reversed and blessings will flow down from heaven to reach the nations. This is a precious promise, but there is an ambiguity here.

The word 'offspring' has a double meaning. Imagine if someone reaches into their wallet and says, 'Let me show you a photo of my offspring'. Until you see the photo, you don't know whether they've got one child or a clutch. 'Offspring' can mean one child, or it can mean a whole clan! It's a word that could be singular or plural.

So what does it mean that Abraham is promised 'offspring'? Well, on the one hand we are reminded of the single offspring first mentioned in Genesis 3:15— the serpent-crushing Saviour. On the other hand it could mean *many* offspring—a multitude. We should hold both meanings together. In God's plan, *many* offspring would come from Abraham—the nation of Israel. But from that nation, the one Offspring would come—Christ. Christ, as King of the Jews, would come from the nation and he would represent the nation. In this way the offspring of Abraham—both plural and singular—would save the world.

What was God doing with such a promise? He was establishing a messianic people, a new humanity— not an eastward, upward people, but a westward, downward people. This new people would no longer wander in exile. Instead they were called back into friendship. And through Abraham's offspring all of heaven's blessings would flow down to the nations of the earth.

In Genesis 12 we see God's global concern and his particular people. God wants to bless 'all nations of the earth' (Gen. 12:3), but he will do it through the offspring of Abraham. So begins the Old Testament's focus on Israel. From here until the New Testament we watch just one nation and their relationship with God. But this does not mean God is ignoring the other nations. God's purpose in it all is to bless the world, but to do it *through* this special people—the people of the Messiah.

After much difficulty, Abraham and his wife, Sarah, finally have a son, Isaac (see Gen. 15–18). So now picture the boy Isaac, smiling in the family photograph. What are you looking at? In a literal sense you are looking at Abraham's offspring—the future of the human race! In Isaac lies a whole people (Israel) and in that people lies the Messiah. When you look at Isaac you're considering the hope of the *world*! If you had to raise this promised offspring, can you imagine how protective you would be?

But Genesis chapter 22 springs an almighty shock!

## KILL ME A SON

> Oh God said to Abraham, 'Kill me a son'
> Abe says, 'Man, you must be puttin' me on'
> God say, 'No'. Abe say, 'What?'…
> —*Highway 61 Revisited*

This is Bob Dylan's re-telling of the story. Dylan hasn't exactly reported *Abraham's* reaction here. Instead he puts words to *our* feelings. *What?!!*

Because in Genesis 22, God says:

> Take your son, your only son, Isaac, whom you love, and go to the region of Moriah. Sacrifice him there

as a burnt offering on one of the mountains I will tell you about. (Gen. 22:2)

And we all want to say 'Man, you must be puttin' me on!'

How on earth are we meant to understand this story? Written in a holy book no less? What's the moral supposed to be, 'Go and do likewise'?

No. If we copied or endorsed each and every practice recorded in the Bible we'd be in a terrible mess. Genesis 22 is meant to be read the way the whole Bible is meant to be read—first and foremost it is a biography. It testifies to *Jesus*. And when we read it this way, the whole thing becomes clear.

## TESTIMONY TO JESUS

Think about this scene. Isaac is Abraham's offspring. He is described as 'the only beloved son'. He stands at the head of a blessed people but he himself is meant to be sacrificed. He's going to be a 'burnt offering' which is a sacrifice of 'atonement'—i.e. it's a sacrifice to make God and man 'at one'. And the place of this sacrifice is a mountain in 'the region of Moriah'. Mount Moriah is the temple mount of Jerusalem (2 Chron. 3:1). What's more, verse 6 tells us that the father carries the tools of judgement (the fire and the knife), while the beloved son ascends the hill carrying the wood of the sacrifice on his back. As we view this mountain, we're meant to think of another.

I was once teaching this story to teenagers and built up the picture layer by layer: 'He is the only

47

beloved son—remind you of anyone? He's the hope of the world, the source of all blessing—sound familiar? He's trudging up the hill with wood on his back— remind you of anything? It's a hill in the region of Jerusalem—ring any bells? It's going to be a sacrifice of atonement—know what I mean?' Suddenly, for a girl in the front row, the penny drops. She starts thumping her friend—really thumping her—with the kind of violence born of pure joy: 'Oh my gosh, oh my gosh, oh my gosh. It's Jesus! It's Jesus! It's totally Jesus!'

That, essentially, is why the Bible was written. It was written to make us say 'Oh my gosh, it's Jesus, it's totally Jesus!' When we read the Scriptures like this, they start to make sense. Instead of Genesis 22 being an insurmountable barrier to faith, when we see that it testifies to Jesus it becomes an incredible boost to faith. Remember that Genesis 22 records an event two millennia before Christ was crucified! But, from the beginning, the Bible has always been testifying to this central event in human history.

## GOD WILL PROVIDE

In verse 8 Isaac asks his father about the sacrifice. Abraham replies: 'God himself will provide the lamb for the burnt offering.' Abraham's faith is being sorely tested. But he believes that God will provide a sacrificial lamb. *Somehow* a substitute will be provided. *Somehow* God will offer a lamb and everything will be OK.

The tension builds. No sign of an intervention.
They reach the top and Abraham ties up his son. We
cannot imagine the looks in their eyes. There has
never been a test of faith like this one. But Abraham
trusts that *somehow* God will bring Isaac through this.
After all, Isaac is his promised offspring, the hope of
the world. Even if he has to go through death, God
will raise him up (Heb. 11:17-19).

And so Abraham lays Isaac on the altar. We all
hold our collective breaths. And then... the Angel of
the Lord intervenes (v.11). We sigh with relief.

Abraham spots an animal caught in the thicket.
Here is a sacrifice to be made instead of Isaac (v.13).
But, crucially, this isn't the 'lamb' that God promised.
On this occasion Abraham kills a *ram*. The 'lamb'
must yet be future. This is why the whole episode
ends like this:

> Abraham called that place The LORD Will Provide.
> And to this day it is said, 'On the mountain of the
> LORD it will be provided.' (Gen. 22:14)

Notice the future tense. The Lord *will* provide. What
will the Lord provide? The Lamb of God, the Offspring of Abraham, the Beloved Son, the Hope of the
world. One day, on that very mountain, God would
provide the ultimate atonement. And the people knew
it. For centuries afterwards they would point to that
hill and say: 'The true sacrifice is coming, and that's
where he'll be provided!'

## WHAT'S IT ALL ABOUT?

God did not ask Abraham to go through with the sacrifice. But one day God would provide. He would offer his Beloved to the world. On a dark Friday 2000 years later, the Son of God willingly walked up that hill, carrying the wood on his back. The Messiah stood at the head of his people and he died to make atonement.

This is what the Bible is about. The Scriptures are not an ancient history lesson or an ethical handbook. Not ultimately. If we attempt to read the Bible primarily as a rule-book, it crumbles between our fingers. With such a mindset, Genesis 22 is a scandal and a barrier to faith.

Yet when the Bible is read as intended we see it as a testimony to Christ. At that point Genesis 22 becomes not a barrier but a boost to faith. Suddenly we realise that all the Bible and all believers in every age are fixed on the one truth that towers above all others:

Look, the Lamb of God, who takes away the sin of the world. (John 1:29)

*Keep reading...*

Genesis 22
Exodus 12
Isaiah 53

*Keep thinking...*

Over thousands of years the Bible reveals an incredible consistency. How do you respond to the amazing accuracy of these prophecies?

Do you see the difference between reading the Bible as a rule-book and reading it as a testimony to Jesus? How would that affect the way you read the Bible?

How does Genesis 22 enrich your understanding of Jesus and his death?

# 4
# Burning Bush

'I guess I'm waiting for my burning bush experience.'

I've met several people who have told me this. They don't yet believe and they can't imagine believing until they are confronted with something truly awe-inspiring—a burning bush experience is often what they'll call it. It's thought of as an earth-shattering occurrence, an epic spiritual encounter, a profound wake-up call to heavenly reality.

But think about what the burning bush actually was. In the book of Exodus, Moses is herding some sheep in a desert place and he encounters... drumroll... some flaming shrubbery. It's not the most overwhelming sight in the world, is it? Later in the book of Exodus there are some properly impressive miracles: magical showdowns, plagues of biblical proportions, thundering mountains and Red Sea crossings.

But blazing botany? Not so inspiring, is it? So why is this the launch event for the Exodus? Surely the

Lord's PR company could come up with something better. It's not like there were any budget constraints. Why did the Lord choose a burning bush to transform Moses' life? And why do we speak of 'burning bush events' transforming modern lives? Isn't the burning bush a little passé to be considered significant?

No. Once we understand its symbolism we'll see that encountering a burning bush is the most transformative event imaginable. It can change any life. Whether you are sceptical, suffering, sinful, sick, sad or just plain stuck, the burning bush is the answer. It's what the whole world needs.

To explain why, we need to go back a few centuries...

## DOWN INTO EGYPT

In about 2000 BC (give or take), Abraham had been promised 'offspring'. As we've already seen 'offspring' has a double-meaning. It could mean one particular descendant or it could mean many—a whole nation. In the Bible, both meanings are in view when we think of 'Abraham's offspring'.

On the one hand we might think of Abraham's many descendants—the nation of Israel. Certainly they are a blessed people—blessed by God in order to be a blessing for the world.

But we can also think of 'Abraham's offspring' in singular terms. After all, Adam and Eve had been promised a particular offspring back in Genesis 3—one who would crush the serpent and save the world. Therefore 'the offspring' makes us think of Christ.

When we read of 'Abraham's offspring' we should have both these meanings in mind (cf Gal. 3:16, 29). We should look at Israel, the many descendants of Abraham, and we should see them as 'God's son' (cf. Exod. 4:22-23; Hosea 11:1). They are his pride and joy. But in all that happens to them we are seeing a prefigurement of Christ, the true Offspring, the eternal Son. Israel is Jesus-shaped and vice versa.

That's important because when we get to Genesis 15 we are told the shape of that life:

> Then the LORD said to [Abraham], 'Know for certain that for four hundred years your descendants [literally *your offspring*] will be strangers in a country not their own and that they will be enslaved and ill-treated there. But I will punish the nation they serve as slaves, and afterwards they will come out with great possessions.' (Gen. 15:13–14)

Here is a prediction of the Exodus given half a millennium in advance. Abraham's offspring will be enslaved then liberated. They will be in bondage in Egypt and then come out 'with great possessions'. The life of Abraham's offspring will take this shape: down then up; to darkness then light; into suffering then out to a greater glory.

Even before Abraham had *any* children, the Lord prophesies the affliction of his people. Abraham's offspring *would* make good... eventually. But only after centuries of misery. This is always the way with God's people—first suffering, then glory. That shape will be important as we explore the Exodus story.

## FROM ABRAHAM TO MOSES

After the prediction of Genesis 15, Abraham's off-spring—the nation of Israel—begins to grow. First comes Isaac; then his son Jacob. Jacob has twelve sons including Joseph, to whom he gives an amazing, technicolour dreamcoat. You may know the story of how Joseph's brothers, consumed by jealousy, sell Joseph into slavery. This is how the Egyptian 'adventure' begins.

Joseph begins at the bottom in Egypt but he prospers, even rising to become prime minister. Here is another example of the old pattern: down then up, darkness then light, suffering then glory. By the end of Genesis, Joseph is ruling Egypt. He is reconciled to his brothers, reunited with his father, and the whole family relocates to Egypt under Joseph's protection.

Time passes and Israel continues to multiply. Once Joseph is dead and long-forgotten, a new Egyptian King (Pharaoh) feels threatened by the Jews. In moves that are chillingly familiar, Pharaoh herds them into labour camps and then the genocide begins. Every newborn Jewish boy is to be drowned in the Nile.

So the ancient prophecy is coming true. Abraham's offspring is enslaved. In their four centuries of affliction the people call to the Lord.

> The Israelites groaned in their slavery and cried out, and their cry for help because of their slavery went up to God. God heard their groaning and he remembered his covenant with Abraham, with Isaac

and with Jacob. So God looked on the Israelites and was concerned about them. (Exod. 2:23-25)

Here are four wonderful verbs: God heard, God remembered, God looked and God was concerned.

And what was God's response? The burning bush.

## GOD TO THE RESCUE

We pick up the story in Exodus chapter 3...

Now Moses was tending the flock of Jethro his father-in-law, the priest of Midian, and he led the flock to the far side of the desert and came to Horeb, the mountain of God. There the angel of the LORD appeared to him in flames of fire from within a bush. Moses saw that though the bush was on fire it did not burn up. So Moses thought, 'I will go over and see this strange sight—why the bush does not burn up.' (Exod. 3:1-3)

If you look closely, you'll see that there are three elements at work here: the bush, the burning and the One in the midst of the flames.

### 1. The bush

Many times in the Bible, the people are described as being like a plant: a vine, branch or tree (cf. Ps. 80; Isa. 5; Isa. 11; Judg. 9). This shrubbery signifies the people as a whole or it refers to their King who represents them. It's in this context that Jesus says to his people, 'I am the vine; you are the branches' (John 15:5).

If you wanted to get technical you could say that the bush stands for the 'offspring of Abraham'. Or, more simply, the bush is the people of God.

## 2. The burning

Many times the suffering of the Israelites in Egypt is pictured as a furnace (Deut. 4:20; 1 Kings 8:51; Jer. 11:4). It's the furnace of affliction.

So now, putting those two elements together, we have a bush that is burning—burning, but not consumed—and, wonder of wonders, the Angel of the Lord comes down *into* the burning bush.

This brings us to the One dwelling in the midst. But who is he?

## 3. The One in the bush

We met the Angel of the Lord in the last chapter. He was the One who intercepted Isaac's sacrifice. In doing so, he both spoke and acted in God's name (Gen. 22:15-17). In fact the Angel always speaks and acts in God's name. He speaks divine words, performs divine acts, makes divine oaths, claims divine titles and receives divine worship. In this very chapter he is called 'the Lord', 'the God of Abraham', and the great 'I AM'. Each and every time he appears in the Bible (and he appears often), he comes as a kind of God-from-God. He *is* the Lord and yet he's *of* the Lord, sent on a divine mission.

At this point it should be said that the title 'The Angel of the Lord' should not make us think of a rosy-cheeked, Justin-Bieber-with-wings. The word

'Angel' does not mean 'creature'. It means 'sent one'. So the title 'The Angel of the LORD' literally means 'The One Sent from the LORD'. He *is* the LORD and he is *of* the LORD. He comes as the Sent One who reveals the Sender in divine glory.

Once we remember that these are precisely the ways Jesus introduces himself in the New Testament ('the one sent from the Father') we realise who this is. The Angel of the Lord is Christ, the Son of God. He is the One who the Father always sends to accomplish his work. In the fullness of time he would be sent as the promised Offspring, the Messiah. But even before he becomes a man, he reveals his eternal nature. It is always his nature to come down, to enter into our affliction and to be with us in the furnace.

## WHEN GOD SHOWS UP

Towards the end of the Old Testament there is another famous story where the Angel appears (Dan. 3:28). Three Israelites are being persecuted for their faith—thrown into 'a burning fiery furnace' (Dan. 3:6, KJV). Yet as the King consigns them to certain death, he is astonished to peer into the furnace and see not three figures but four. The old King James translation captures the scene memorably:

> Lo, I see four men loose, walking in the midst of the fire, and they have no hurt; and the form of the fourth is like the Son of God. (Dan. 3:25, KJV)

In verse 28, the King identifies this figure as the Angel of God. He is the Son whose nature is always to come down, to enter the flames and to bring us out.

This is what we see in the burning bush: not a flame-proof tree but a flame-bound God—one who joins us in the furnace. What arrests Moses' attention is not a heavenly spectacle but unfathomable love. He's not the God that we expected. But he's exactly the God we need.

In Exodus, the Son of God came down to be with his people and to lead them out. In the New Testament he descended even further, not just to a burning bush, but he entered into our humanity for all time. He took our sorrows and sufferings on himself. Then, in the end, he took our sins on himself. On the cross he endured the flames that were destined for us.

Moses saw Christ in a burning bush. We see him on a wooden cross, but it's the same person with the same redeeming love. And from the midst of his fiery affliction we can hear him say what he said to Moses:

> I have indeed seen the misery of my people... I have heard them crying out... and I am concerned about their suffering. So I have come down to rescue them. (Exod. 3:7-8)

## WHAT WOULD MAKE YOU BELIEVE?

A burning bush experience is meant to wake us up to heavenly reality. So what kind of God is revealed in the burning bush? Not simply a power above us but a saviour with us.

Centuries after the exodus, the prophet Isaiah reflected back on the burning bush in these words:

> In all their affliction [God] too was afflicted,
>     and the angel of his presence saved them;
> in his love and in his pity he redeemed them;
>     he lifted them up and carried them all the
> days of old. (Isa. 63:9, ESV)

Here is a God who not only gains our assent, but wins our hearts. He doesn't so much give proofs—he gives himself. Moses memorialised the God of Israel as '[he] who dwelt in the burning bush' (Deut. 33:16). Here is a God we can believe in.

*Keep reading…*

Exodus 1:1–2:10
Exodus 2:11–3:22
1 Corinthians 1:18–2:5

*Keep thinking…*

How do people generally look for 'proofs' of God? What kind of gods would be proven in these ways?

What kind of God does the One in the burning bush reveal? How does this help us when we think about God and suffering?

What links can you see between the burning bush and the cross?

# 5
# Thou Shalt

One summer some friends of mine went on holiday and offered their house to a family they didn't really know. After a fortnight away, my friends returned to find a four page letter from the summer occupants. The letter comprised one page of thank yous and three pages itemising the breakages. That's quite a list. I'm not sure I have three pages-worth of things to break, but if I did I think I'd want to lay down the law a little more forcefully to my house guests.

That's often something you do when you invite people into your house—at least if they're going to stay a while. For the smooth running of family life, you make sure everyone knows the house rules. It's not because you want to exclude them from things, it's actually because you want them to be a part of your home life. This is what God does to *his* household.

In Exodus chapter 4, God calls Israel his 'son' (Exod. 4:22-23). The rest of Exodus shows how God saves his son out of slavery and welcomes him home.

It's *then*, from chapter 20, that he teaches Israel some family manners. Let's see how it happened.

## FROM BURNING BUSH TO BLAZING MOUNTAIN

As our last chapter ended, the Exodus story was just getting started. At the burning bush the Lord commissions Moses to lead his people out of slavery. That's what the word 'exodus' means: 'way out'. It's all about how God stoops to our plight to give us a way out.

In Exodus 3:12, the One in the bush tells Moses the plan:

> I will be with you. And this will be the sign to you that it is I who have sent you: when you have brought the people out of Egypt, you will worship God on this mountain.

Here is the great I AM (v. 14), the One whose nature is always to come down. He descended to the burning bush in Exodus 3, he descended to the fiery furnace in Daniel 3, and he descended to our fiery affliction in the Gospels. This is how the great I AM always works. To those trapped in the darkness, the Son comes to be with us, to be for us, and to carry us home to the Father. We are not saved in order to be independent; we are saved for fellowship—saved into the Father's family.

From Exodus chapter 5, we read of how Moses and his brother Aaron confront Pharaoh, the Egyptian king. They bring God's famous demand: 'Let my people go'. Pharaoh, who very much plays the Satan figure in this story, scoffs at the Jews and their trust in the Lord. Pharaoh requires some fairly spectacular 'persuasion' in order to heed God's call. This is where the 'plagues of biblical proportions' come in (Exod. 7–12). Ten fearful judgements fall, each worse than the last, until finally there comes the plague on the firstborn. The Lord will strike down the firstborn son of every household, whether Egyptian or Israelite. In the face of such judgement there was just one way of escape: kill a lamb and paint the blood on the doorposts. The Lord would 'pass over' any household that trusted in the blood of the lamb, hence the name 'Passover'.

As the Israelites took part in this ritual no doubt they were reminded of Abraham and Isaac 500 years earlier—reminded that 'God will provide' the atoning lamb. In Exodus 12 we see another angle on what the Lamb would do when he came in the fullness of time: he would be sacrificed and his blood would allow God's judgement to 'pass over' us. The Passover is just one more way the events of the Old Testament prefigured those of the New.

Through this final plague, God's people were saved. Pharaoh let the Israelites go but then, typically, he had a change of heart. Slaves are valuable, after all. Pharaoh sent his armies to retrieve his property which was headed out of Egypt. The scrambling Israelites were cornered by the Red Sea with no way forwards and Egyptian chariots hemming them in. It looked like the God who had saved them through the blood of the lamb was not able to complete the rescue. That is until Moses parted the Red Sea. Or rather the Spirit of God parted the Red Sea through Moses (Exod. 14:21-22). In this way the Israelites pass through. The Egyptians murderously pursue the Israelites even though it had become obvious that they were fighting God himself. They chased death and found it. The waters that looked to be the death of the Israelites became the grave of their enemies. Israel was saved, Egypt was judged, and the promises of God were fulfilled.

Having brought Israel out of bondage, the great I AM was true to his promise. Having delivered his people, he brought them back to the same mountain to worship God.

## HOUSE RULES

Notice the order of things. God did not lay down the law in Egypt. He did not tell his people 'You're slaves but if you learn to obey my laws I'll make you my son.' No, they *are* God's son and he saves them before and apart from any obedience they might have offered him. They are saved by the sheer mercy of God.

But now that they're part of the family, it's time for 'God's son' to learn family manners. As God's pride and joy, Israel is now told what the life of God's son looks like. We often call these 'the Ten Commandments' but more literally they are 'Ten Words'—ten expressions of the life of God's son.

Let me paraphrase what you can read for yourself in Exodus 20:1-17:

1. You will trust me as your Protector and Provider.

2. You won't look to other things as your ultimate source of life and joy.

3. You'll represent my character faithfully to the world. You won't use my name as a rubber stamp for your own agenda.

4. You'll take a day off each week to show that life and salvation comes from me, not from your own efforts.

5. You'll honour those closest to you, starting with your parents.

6. You won't murder.

7. You won't commit adultery.

8. You won't steal.

9. You won't lie.

10. You won't look greedily at the things of this world. You'll be content with me and what I have for you.

These are the ten words expressing the life of God's son. What do you think of them?

I think if we're seeing things clearly we realise that this is 'the Good Life'. This, surely, is life as it's meant to be lived.

It's all about love. That's how Jesus summarised the Old Testament law. When questioned about how to view the law he said it all boils down to this: 'Love God' and 'Love your neighbour' (Matt. 22:35-40). The law describes the life of love.

And there's a flow to this life. Essentially the first four commandments are about love for God and the last six are about love for others. Therefore, a right relationship with God is meant to flow out into a right relationship with the world. It's a beautiful vision for life.

When Jesus came in the flesh he said he had come to 'fulfil the law' (Matt. 5:17). The Old Testament law was the life of God's son written down, but Jesus in the New Testament shows the life of God's Son in the flesh. And when we saw it lived out we witnessed an incomparable life of grace, truth and utter self-giving. Having seen the law lived out in Jesus we can see just how wonderful God's Good Life is. But that leaves us with a question...

## HOW DO I MEASURE UP?

I can't deny that the law describes the Good Life. But does it describe *my* life? Do these family manners come naturally to me? Do I live the way of God's son?

Before we rush to reply, consider this: the law is more than skin deep. It goes to the heart. Think for instance of the tenth commandment: 'You will not covet'. That means 'don't be jealous of other people's stuff'. It's about my thought-life. It's about what captivates my *heart*. If I covet my neighbour's flat-screen TV, I am guilty of breaking the law whether or not I lie, steal or kill to get it.

The Good Life described by the law gets under our skin. It cuts to our core. Let me show you how. Look at the list of commandments above and pick the two that are easiest to keep. Which two can most people claim to have *fully* obeyed throughout their lives?

I'm guessing you've chosen commandments 6 and 7. 'Don't murder' and 'Don't commit adultery'. After all, these are pretty clear. You've either committed homicide or you haven't. You've either cheated on your spouse or you haven't, right?

But Jesus goes much deeper than this. He refers back to the ten commandments and says that anyone 'who is angry' has broken the sixth commandment (Matt. 5:22). And 'whoever looks… lustfully' has broken the seventh (Matt. 5:28). Murder and adultery are matters of anger and lust—matters *of the heart*. Instead of being the easiest commandments to tick off, they are actually some of the most convicting standards ever espoused in the history of ethics.

When you think about it, much of our lives is driven by lust and anger. We *want* things—often illicitly (think of the tenth commandment). And as we pursue such things we open ourselves up to anger because so often we can't attain them, or others stand in our way, or we manage to get them and then they fail to satisfy us. Life is a constant swirl of lust and anger. And those are the two 'easiest' commands to obey!

So what do we think of these ten words? Can any of us still claim to have lived the Good Life?

I'll confess for myself—I have failed spectacularly at all ten. Even the most apparently simple of commandments convict me of profound moral failure. This whole description of the Good Life proclaims me 'guilty'.

I don't naturally trust my heavenly Father as Protector and Provider. So my heart goes after other things. I covet and I lust. Then, in that deep and terrible sense that Jesus means, I'll lie, steal and even kill to get what I want. From mistrust, to lust, to murderous anger my heart condemns me.

## WHAT'S THE ANSWER?

If this is the problem, what is the solution?

Most people say this:

> Yes you've messed up. But nobody's perfect. Pick yourself back up. Get wise. Choose right. Try hard. Keep going. Will-power will save you!

But there's a problem with such pep-talks. They don't work. They are simply more laws for me to obey. They only add to the pile of commands I manage to break. At times they may change my outward behaviour. But they don't get to the root of the problem. These 'thou shalts' might *describe* a life of love. They might urge me towards it. But they can't *produce* that love.

Not convinced? I'll prove it. Allow me to command you, in the name of the Lord: *Love God!*

Did it work? Were you able to muster up heart-felt devotion for God? Of course not. Love can't be commanded. Therefore more laws, more will-power, and more pep-talks can't be the answer.

Yet the world is full of religions, philosophies, seminars, best-selling paperbacks, life-style gurus, and so on. They've all got visions of the Good Life. But, at the end of the day, they are just another set of commandments.

Next time you're at a magazine stand, browse the magazine covers. Count up all the commandments that blare at you in bold-type. 'Wage war on fat'. 'Eleven carbs you should eat'. 'Improve your game'. 'De-clutter your life'. The world is *full* of 'thou shalts'. And every one of them represents an expectation that *I* can pull off the Good Life. All of them are asking *me* to make it happen. But I'll be honest: I can't do it.

Even *God's* law can't make me good. Even God's law with God's *help* won't do it. Even when I'm really trying, I just can't live up to the life that I know is right. In fact nothing shows up my badness like a concerted effort at goodness.

When the people at mount Sinai heard the law they agreed that it was good. They agreed that it was binding on them. And within a matter of days they burst out in a drunken orgy and began to worship false gods (Exod. 32). On one level it's shocking. On another it's completely predictable. The law is good but we are not. The more law, the more pressure. The more pressure, the more we rebel. I see it in others. I see it in myself. Even when I want to, I *don't* live the life of God's son. And on a very deep level I *can't* live the life of God's son.

This is serious. We were created to share in the family life of God! Yet none of us live the life of God's child. This means we don't belong in the one household we were made for. It's not so much that my *law-breaking* doesn't belong to the life of God. *I* don't belong. It's not simply about broken rules, it's about our broken humanity. The law shows up my disordered and dark heart. It reveals that I have no right to belong to God's family.

That's the bad news. And there's no commandment, principle or programme that can fix it. Even the very best teaching about the very best life will not help. The problem is *me*. And the solution is out of my hands.

But next we'll see what God has done about that.

*Keep reading…*

> Exodus 20:1-20
> Matthew 5:17-48
> Romans 3:9-31

*Keep thinking…*

What experiences have you had of people 'laying down the law'? Has it ever had the opposite effect, tempting you to *break* the rules instead?

How do you feel about the Good Life as outlined in the Ten Commandments? How do you feel you measure up?

If we have a problem with living the Good Life, is the solution to have more or better laws? If not, what do you think is the answer?

# 6

# Scapegoat

We don't like the idea of 'scapegoating'. It sounds like bullying. Mostly, when we hear about it, it's a case of a group picking on a weakling. They identify all their problems with this one individual and they punish the scapegoat for the sins of the community.

Have you ever been scapegoated? It wasn't your fault but the blame fell on you.

It happens in families—you're the 'problem child' and the family takes it out on you. You can never do things right. No matter how you act or speak, your siblings roll their eyes, your parents get exasperated.

It happens in organisations—your department is unfairly singled out for blame by your employer. You have to 'take the hit' and step down from a society or political party.

It happens in cultures—society's sick and apparently your kind are the problem. Perhaps you're an immigrant or from the wrong tribe or a single mother or disabled, or... the list goes on. The scapegoat is blamed for all our ills. It is punished, shunned, thrust out of the community as the mob cries: 'Good riddance to bad rubbish'.

Scapegoating in the modern sense is horrific. But it's horrific because of the power relationship: the strong are sacrificing the weak. In the Bible, the 'scapegoat' was teaching something very different.

## THE LAW AND THE SCAPEGOAT

The Bible's teaching about the scapegoat comes in the context of the law—that package of commandments that begins with 'thou shalt'. We thought about this in the last chapter: 'Thou shalts' describe the life of God's son. They paint for us a compelling picture of the Good Life. Just imagine a world of perfect love: love for God and love for neighbour. The law depicts this world—the world we all want. It's the kind of life where trust in God flows out into care for others. When we appreciate the law we have two reactions. First, we say to ourselves, 'Yes! This is how life is meant to be lived.' But hot on the heels of that response we say, 'No! This is not what comes out of my heart.' In the law there's goodness, but in me there's badness. This is a problem.

But the law also points to a way out. Alongside the 'thou shalts', the law points to the solution to sin. It's an elaborate, interactive, multi-media presentation called the tabernacle.

## THE TABERNACLE

The tabernacle was a tent (later rebuilt as the temple) which acted as a portable model of heaven and earth. Through the tabernacle a grand drama was enacted, one which tells the story of how bad people can still meet with a good God.

At the heart of the tabernacle was the inner sanctum, called the 'holy of holies'. It contained 'the ark of the covenant', a gold-plated box which held the ten commandments. This ark was the throne of the Lord. God's own Good Life was the very atmosphere of this space. But for that reason it was impossible for sinners to be there. To call the holy of holies 'off limits' is like calling a nuclear bunker 'secluded'. No-one could enter this throne room except the High Priest and only on one day of the year and only after some *very* elaborate rituals. Everything about this structure was screaming to the Israelites 'keep out'.

If the holy of holies was the centre of the temple, radiating out from the centre were spaces that became *slightly* more accessible. Next to the holy of holies was 'the holy place'—divided from the holy of holies by a thick curtain. Only a special cast of elite priests could enter the holy place, but again, only on the basis of elaborate rituals. Outside the holy place stood a basin and an altar, reminders that these special priests could only access God through cleansing and atoning sacrifices.

As we move out again we reach the court of Israel where ordinary Israelites could come to confess their sins and make their sacrifices. And moving out some more we find the court of the Gentiles where non-Jews could peer in and see *something* of the outer life of God's holiness.

Everything about the tabernacle was telling you that bad people do not belong with a good God. We are kept at a distance by our sin.

So far, so prohibiting. But that's why over and over Exodus and Leviticus (the book after Exodus) tell us about the priests. It was the priests, and the sacrifices they made, that dramatised the way sinners can get to heaven.

## THE WAY TO GOD

How do you picture the pathway to heaven? Perhaps you imagine a gentle incline, serenity, wisdom, peace and charity. Anyone visiting the tabernacle would see the truth: the way to God is paved with blood! The tabernacle was many things, but it was never less than a slaughterhouse.

If you were a sinner—and the law condemns *everyone* as a sinner—you would come to the tabernacle bringing birds, goats, lambs and bulls. As you come confessing your sins you would lay your hands on the animal's head because you're meant to identify with the sacrifices. You're meant to realise that this animal is getting what you deserve. Then the knives come out. Every day the altar would run over with gallons of animal blood.

We still have slaughterhouses today of course. Every day animals die so that we might live. It's just that, back in the Old Testament, your butcher (a.k.a. your priest) was also giving you a spiritual lesson. Before the animal was dinner it was a teaching point: Life comes through death. That is physically true, of course, but at the tabernacle you were urged to consider this on a deeper level. *Spiritual* life also requires a death. It ought to be you that gets it in the neck. But your sacrifice dies instead.

Perhaps we read this and cry out: What did those poor animals ever do to deserve death?! Actually, that's the point. The animals did no wrong. You sinned. The sacrifice paid for you—and paid in blood. The innocent dies for the guilty.

Of course none of these rituals *actually* dealt with sin. It was all a dramatization. It only modelled to the ancient people what the true Lamb of God would do when he came. But it was a powerful teaching.

Just as the 'Thou shalts' described the *life* of God's Son, so the tabernacle described the *death* of God's Son. And just as the commandments show us our sin, so the sacrifices show us our salvation. Every death was pointing to Christ's ultimate death on the cross— that was the death that would make God and sinners 'at one'.

There was one day in particular that demonstrated this truth. It was called the Day of Atonement. This was the day when, through sacrifice, the people could celebrate their at-one-ment with God.

## THE DAY OF ATONEMENT

On this one day in early Autumn, the High Priest brought two goats to the tabernacle in front of all the people.

> [Aaron, the High Priest] is to cast lots for the two goats—one lot for the LORD and the other for the scapegoat. Aaron shall bring the goat whose lot falls to the LORD and sacrifice it for a sin offering. But the goat chosen by lot as the scapegoat shall be presented alive before the LORD to be used for making atonement by sending it into the desert as a scapegoat. (Lev. 16:8-10)

These two goats will represent different aspects of Christ's sacrifice. One goat is designated 'the LORD', and he's killed. What a fearful duty for the High Priest to put a knife to the neck of 'the LORD'!

The other goat is labelled the scapegoat. And here's what Aaron does with this goat:

> He is to lay both hands on the head of the live goat and confess over it all the wickedness and rebellion of the Israelites—all their sins—and put them on the goat's head. He shall send the goat away into the desert in the care of a man appointed for the task. The goat will carry on itself all their sins to a solitary place; and the man shall release it in the desert. (Lev. 16:21-22)

Through the two goats, two aspects of the cross are being shown. First, Christ the Lord will die for our sins. But secondly, in his death, he will carry our sins far away.

## CHRIST OUR SCAPEGOAT

If you want to understand the death of Jesus, imagine this:

You are an ancient worshipper who knows your sinfulness, so you bring your sacrifice to the tabernacle. As you wait in the queue a voice comes from the Holy of Holies. It's the Lord. He says, 'Get out!'

The priests hitch up their robes and start running. They usher you away to a safe distance. The Lord climbs down from his throne and strides out into the courtyard. You are terrified. There you are, confessing to be a sinner. And there he is, the Almighty Lord!

But incredibly, he doesn't come to judge. Instead of flinging you on the altar, he lays on it himself. A priest is called over to confess the sins of the people. He does so, laying his hands of the Lord's head.

Then, carrying the sins of all the people, the great I AM is slain. As his blood is spilled your sins are cleansed away forever. This is what happened when Christ came and died. Jesus was our Scapegoat, sacrificed for the sins of the world.

This is why the *Bible's* teaching about the scapegoat is the reverse of our modern notions of scapegoating. When the *Lord* takes on the role of Scapegoat it's not the oppression of the weak. It's the willing sacrifice of the strong. We mustn't scapegoat others. We ought to be responsible—responsible enough to confess our sins, and lay them on Christ.

*He* atones for our sins. Not the blood of *animals*. Not even the blood of people. What pays for our sins is the blood of God himself offered on the cross (Acts 20:28).

## OFFLOADING OUR SINS

Charles Simeon was an English preacher in the late eighteenth and early nineteenth centuries. In his younger years he was weighed down by a heavy sense of sin. Where could he find relief for his soul and forgiveness with God?

When he heard that Christ was offered as his Scapegoat, Simeon made the breakthrough:

> What! May I transfer all my guilt to another? Has God provided an offering for me, that I may lay my sins on his Head? Then, God willing, I will not bear them on my own soul one moment longer. Accordingly I sought to lay my sins upon the sacred head of Jesus.

All of us carry sins. All of us fail to be the people we know we should be, and there is nothing we can do to atone for ourselves. Our sins demand, not merely the blood of animals, not even the blood of humans—they have demanded the blood of God! There is nothing we can offer to make atonement.

But then, there's nothing we *need* to offer to make atonement. Christ *has* been sacrificed. And his offering is unconditional, unimprovable and unrepeatable. We can't add to it. We can't take away from it. The only question is, Have we taken advantage of it?

Have you 'laid your sins on the sacred head of Jesus'? Have you identified with Jesus, asking *him* to be your atonement? He died to bear your burdens. Don't you carry them a moment longer. Call out to Jesus and give him your sins. It is his glory to take them, to pay for them and to remove them from you entirely.

As far as the east is from the west, so far has he removed our transgressions from us. (Ps. 103:12)

*Keep reading...*

Leviticus 16:1-34
Hebrews 9:1-28
Hebrews 10:1-25

*Keep thinking...*

In the Bible, there's a Scapegoat to carry our sins. What do you do with yours?

Atonement is a bloody thing. Why do you think that is?

The cross is basically the Lord being sacrificed on the altar. How do you react to such an atonement?

What did it mean for the Israelites to lay their hands on the sacrifice? What would it mean for you to 'lay your hands on Jesus' head'? Have you done it?

# 7

# Land of Milk and Honey

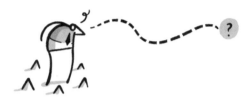

This world will kill you. It could be fires, floods or famines; it could be winds, waves or wars; it could be killers, cars or cancer; it could be disasters, diseases or decay, but one way or another this world will take you down. The doors are locked. No-one gets out of here alive.

I don't mean to sound alarmist, but there it is. Ever since the time of Adam, this world has produced 'thorns and thistles for [us]'. That's how Genesis 3, verse 18 put it. Even plant life is shot through with these miniature bayonets, bared and thrust in our general direction. The thorns and thistles are *for us*. Such barbed nasties are not just generally inconvenient; they are intentionally making our lives difficult. There's a significant sense in which this world is against us.

We all feel this in a general sense but the Israelites felt it especially as they toiled away in Egypt. Egypt gave them a heightened sense that this world is not our home. For them, Egypt was a 'house of slavery' and a 'furnace of affliction'. (Exod. 20:2; Is. 48:10).

Perhaps those descriptions resonate with you: 'misery'; 'slavery'; a 'furnace'. But in the midst of these trials, the Lord shows up to promise 'a good and spacious land, a land flowing with milk and honey'. (Exod. 3:8).

This is the future which the great I AM promises. As God's people are rescued from slavery, they are promised, twenty times in the Old Testament, a 'land of milk and honey'. Better than that—it's a land *flowing* with milk and honey. It will gush forth abundantly with luxuries. There will be no more scrounging for the bare necessities. There will be nothing mean or plain about the promised land—it will overflow with fatness and sweetness.

But the journey towards this richness and rest was not straightforward. As the Israelites came through the Red Sea, delivered from their slave-masters once and for all, they did not instantly enter the 'good and spacious land'. In fact they walked out of slavery and into a desert. Here is the way to God's promised future: God's people are not teleported into ease and comfort; they are led through trial and testing. In fact the great majority of the books of Moses—Genesis, Exodus, Leviticus, Numbers and Deuteronomy—are set in the desert.

## WILDERNESS WANDERING

In the desert, Israel is taught many things. They are fed, day by day, with bread from heaven—the 'bread of angels', known as manna. They are led, day and night, by the Lord who personally accompanies them in a pillar of cloud by day and a pillar of fire by night. In the wilderness they must depend on God for everything. But, as so many of God's people have testified throughout the ages, they found that when God was all they had, God was all they needed.

The New Testament looks back on these wilderness wanderings as a portrait of the life of faith (1 Cor. 10:1–9). Every believer is like these Israelites: we have been saved out of our slavery to sin by the great I AM; we are headed for an incredible promised hope; but in the meantime we are in a desert place, struggling with trial and temptation. The way to glory runs through suffering, but thank God we have the sustenance of Christ, our true Bread (John 6:32-51) and the guidance of the Spirit, who accompanies us every step of the way (Gal. 5:25).

## FEAR OF GIANTS OR FORETASTE OF GLORY?

The journey through the wilderness should have been brief. All they needed to do was keep the Mediterranean on their left and they'd be in the land of milk and honey in about two weeks. But mistrust was their undoing. In Numbers chapter 13, the Israelites are on the brink of the promised land. Moses sends twelve spies to go ahead of them and investigate the land (one for each of the twelve tribes of Israel). Ten of the spies bring back fearful tales of the giants that stalk the land. They urge the people to turn back.

Two of the spies, named Joshua and Caleb, bring back a cluster of grapes—a taste of the land's rich bounty. They say: 'We should go up and take possession of the land, for we can certainly do it' (Num. 13:30).

What would Israel do? Which report of the land would capture their hearts: fear of giants or a foretaste of glory? Tragically the people say: 'We should choose a leader [i.e. another leader, not Moses,] and go back to Egypt' (Num. 14:4). The size of their foes loomed larger in their thinking than the promises of God, than his presence with them, than the future he had sworn to give them. So they shrink back in mistrust and fear.

In response God gives them what they want. Rather than force them against their will into the promised land, God honours their wishes, vowing that none of that generation would enter the land of milk and honey. Of those over 20 years old, only Joshua and Caleb, the two faithful spies, would ever see the land. And so Israel wandered the desert for forty years until the faithless generation died out.

## THE LAW-GIVER AND THE SAVIOUR

Perhaps you're thinking, What about Moses? Would he too perish in the wilderness? Yes, Moses too. Not even he would make it to the land of Canaan. After forty years of wilderness wandering (see the book of Numbers), and having preached his heart out to the nation (see the book of Deuteronomy), Moses climbs to the top of Mount Pisgah, looks out over the land of milk and honey and dies.

Moses, the law-giver, could not enter into the promised hope. But Joshua, his successor, could. 'Joshua' means 'Saviour'. Indeed the name 'Joshua' is the name 'Jesus'. It's just that 'Joshua' is translated directly from Hebrew and 'Jesus' comes from the Greek. The one called 'Jesus' would in fact lead Israel into the land of milk of honey. Hot on his heels would be the other faithful spy, Caleb. 'Caleb' means 'man after his heart'. So then 'Jesus' can enter glory together with the one after his heart.

This preaches to us today. The law won't get us to heaven. All the trappings of religion and ritual will leave us short. The old must die. We don't trust in Moses. He falls short of glory, but Jesus will bring us home.

## ENTERING THE LAND

The first five books of the Bible—Genesis, Exodus, Leviticus, Numbers and Deuteronomy—are often called the Law ('Torah' in Hebrew). They conclude with the death of Moses. Next comes the book of Joshua which details how Joshua led God's people into the land of milk and honey.

There was only one problem with this plan: the land was occupied, and occupied by a ruthless people. Those ten spies weren't joking about the giants. The land of Canaan was full of military super-powers. As the Israelites approached the first military installation called Jericho, onlookers would have been bemused by the scene. Israel was led by a pensioner and possessed virtually zero military training or experience. Their chief weapons seemed to be furniture from the tabernacle and they launched their attacks not with horses and chariots but with priests and musicians. In other words, Israel was pathetic.

Sometimes people dive into the book of Joshua without context and read with alarm of holy war. But that would be like coming in late to Star Wars, watching the Death Star get destroyed and saying 'How awful! What wanton destruction!' No, there's a context in which these things make sense.

Right back in Genesis 15, the Lord promised the land to Abraham's offspring. Even then he spoke of the evils of the inhabitants. Canaanite cultures were involved in child-burning and other grotesque evils (Gen. 15:13-16; cf. 'Molech', Lev. 18:21). Today, if a dictator is found to be killing off innocent members of his own country, the international community may give him four days, four weeks or even four months to stop. The Lord gave the Canaanites four centuries to repent of their evil—considerably longer than any other 'just war' ever launched. When God's 400 years of patience run out he judges that culture through Israel. It's nothing to do with nationality and everything to do with sin (Israel is judged similarly when it falls into the same evils).

The relative strengths of the Israelites and Canaanites are worth considering here. Israel was an absolute minnow on the world stage. Next chapter we will study the most famous instance of 'giant killing'—David and Goliath. That story is the paradigm for all holy war stories in the Bible. Israel is

David, the Canaanites are Goliath. Israel should have been crushed by these superpowers. It would be like Malawi starting a fight with America and somehow wiping them off the map. And now imagine that the Malawian army's chief weapon was blowing trumpets while the US armed forces face off against them. This is how Joshua conducts his campaign (see the 'battle' against Jericho in Joshua 6).

Nowhere in the book of Joshua do we read of non-combatants being killed and everywhere, when Canaanites seek mercy from the Israelites, they are spared. In Joshua 2, for instance, we read of Rahab, the Canaanite prostitute, who finds refuge in God's people. In Joshua 9, there is a whole nation—the Gibeonites—who make peace. These people are more than spared. They are adopted into the heart of the nation, honoured and fiercely protected (see Josh. 10 and Matt. 1:5).

Having said all this, these stories are still serious portraits of judgement and they leave a lump in the throat. They are meant to. They speak to us of the Lord's uncompromising character. In the future glory which he promises, there can be no wickedness, no darkness, no coalition with the forces of evil. All such sin must be judged. God's blazing goodness demands it.

In our thinking, we often play two realities off against each other. We imagine that, on the one hand, God has a joy-filled hope to offer, and on the other he has a fearful judgement to exact. We consider these things as opposites. The Bible shows them to be two sides of the same coin. The Lord's fierce commitment to goodness ensures both. The same Joshua who brings rest for his people also brings a final reckoning for the wicked. The land of milk and honey will be a place cleansed of evil.

## OUR NEW JOSHUA

How should we read these old stories? Especially when Jesus, in the New Testament, stands implacably against violence (see Matt. 5:38-48; 26:52-54; Luke 6:27-36; John 18:36). How can he tell us to put down our swords, yet at the same time he's keen we pick up his book? In his book, the Old Testament, we read of several holy wars. How do we understand this?

We need to read about the battles of the Old Testament the same way we read about the laws and rituals of the Old Testament—as shadows fulfilled by the coming of Jesus. Let's consider those three shadows: laws; rituals and battles.

### Laws

As we saw in chapter 6, Moses gave to Israel a series of 'thou shalts' which laid out the life of God's son to them, yet in culture-specific ways. When Jesus came he perfectly lived the life of God's Son in the flesh. He fulfilled the old shadows and now we receive God's law from Christ's hands, rather than directly from Moses.

## Rituals

As we saw in chapter 7, Moses gave to Israel a series of rituals which laid out the *death* of God's Son to them, yet in culture-specific ways. When Jesus came to fulfil the sacrifices—dying as our substitute—he changed the way we approach those rituals. I still need a lamb to make atonement for me, but I don't need one from Moses' flock. Jesus, the Lamb of God, is all the sacrifice I need. Therefore, as with the 'thou shalts', I read those Old Testament practices as precious revelations addressed to Israel. They are not, though, a 'how to' directly addressed to me.

## Battles

In this chapter we have seen Israel as a nation-state making military interventions. But that is not the life that Jesus gives to his followers in the New Testament. Why? Because Jesus fulfilled *all* the temporary structures of the Old Testament, which includes the temple and its priests and sacrifices. It also includes the nation-state with its kings and armies. There is a radical difference when we step into the world of the New Testament.

When the true Joshua, Jesus, entered Jericho in Luke 19, verse 1, he cleansed the land by *reconciling* a wicked sinner called Zacchaeus. You *could* say that Jesus, in Luke 19, rids the earth of an enemy. But he does it by making peace with him. As Abraham Lincoln once said 'I destroy my enemies when I make them my friends'. This is the kind of conquest Jesus makes of Jericho and it's the kind of conquest that takes him to the cross—not to be the perpetrator of violence but to be its chief victim. It's this wrath-bearing mercy which he urges on his followers. Just as Christ died *for* his enemies to make them his friends, so his followers are to conquer the world with forgiveness (Matt. 28:18-20; Col. 1:13-14).

The New Testament views Joshua's ancient wars as types of our own campaign but it is emphatically a campaign of peace (2 Cor. 10:1-5; Eph. 6:10-20). The book of Joshua is never seen as justification for violence. '*Christian* violence' is a contradiction in terms. While the state may take up the sword (Rom. 13:1-5), the Church may not. Because we trust our true Joshua to bring about the future 'land of milk and honey'—because we entrust all spiritual judgement to *him*—the Church has for the world a message of peace. We urge all people to be Rahab. We urge all people to be the Gibeonites, to be reconciled so that they too might find themselves adopted into the heart of God's family, blessed and protected forever.

This is how we find our way home to God's glorious future. Not through the striving of legal obedience, not through the rituals of ancient religion, and not by the sword in worldly strength. We come home through the true Saviour, Jesus. In him we will find our affliction becoming 'a spacious place' and our 'thorns and thistles' turned to 'milk and honey'.

*Keep reading…*

Deuteronomy 8:1-20
Joshua 2:1-24
1 Corinthians 10:1-13

*Keep thinking…*

What place did the future hope of the promised land have in the hearts and minds of the Israelites? What place should it have had? What place does future hope have in your heart and mind?

What was the wilderness teaching the Israelites? What can it teach us?

How do you respond to the culturally specific laws, rituals and battles of the Old Testament? How does the rest of the Bible read them?

# Catch Up 1:
# From Creation to Kings

| | |
|---|---|
| The beginning of the world. And the beginning of God's people, through Abraham, Isaac and Jacob. | Genesis |
| Through Joseph, the people go down into Egypt. Later they are enslaved for 400 years. | Exodus |
| They are brought out by the Lord through Moses. | |
| They wander through the wilderness for 40 years. | Leviticus, Numbers, Deuteronomy |
| Eventually they re-enter the promised land. | Joshua |

| | |
|---|---|
| While back in the land, the Israelites have many different rulers, called 'Judges'. | Judges, Ruth |
| Israel transitions from 'Judges' to 'Kings'. First Saul, then David, then the descendants of David. | 1 Samuel, 2 Samuel, 1 Kings, 2 Kings, 1 Chronicles, 2 Chronicles |

# 8
# Giant Killing

When a little guy takes on a big corporation it's called 'a David and Goliath story'. When a second division football club beats a Premier League team it's called 'giant killing'.

This famous battle from the book of 1 Samuel has become a common metaphor in our culture. It's the story of a teenager, David, who takes on a monstrous opponent, Goliath. Their struggle is man-to-man, but behind each of them stands an army whose fate lies in the hands of their champion. If David wins, the Israelites conquer. If Goliath wins, the Philistines would rule. And against all the odds it's David who fells the giant with nothing more than a slingshot.

We all know what the story's about, don't we? It's about the underdog gritting their teeth and pulling off a surprising victory, right? It's an inspirational tale for anyone up against the odds. Isn't it?

Not quite. 'David and Goliath' teaches something much deeper than that. The key to the story is to understand the hero. Who *is* David?

## THE KING OF THE JEWS

Here's the first thing to realise about David. He's not just a little guy 'punching above his weight'. He's the king—the king of the Jews. Once you know this fact, everything else falls into place. David exists in a long line of promises that stretches both backwards and forwards. Let's first look backwards.

In Genesis 3 the promise of Christ was simply that the offspring of the woman would save the world. That's pretty broad. In Genesis 12 the promise gets narrowed down to Abraham. Then to Isaac his son, then to Jacob *his* son. Messianic expectation was getting more and more specific.

At the end of Genesis we read this prophecy which narrows the promised line down further:

> The sceptre will not depart from [the tribe of] Judah,
> nor the ruler's staff from between his feet,
> until he to whom it belongs shall come
> and the obedience of the nations shall be his.
> (Gen. 49:10, NIV 2011)

Judah was one of Jacob's twelve sons. The picture here is of a line of kings that are descended from Judah. The sceptre, or 'ruler's staff' is being passed from generation to generation within this royal tribe. The last one in line would be the Messiah himself— the One to whom universal obedience is due. So by the end of Genesis, the promise of Christ has been narrowed down significantly. It's the King of the Jews that will save the world.

If an Israelite saw a king from the line of Judah they would be thinking *Is this the One? Or are they merely a throne warmer for the One?* Certainly the King of the Jews was meant to build anticipation for the Universal King. If they were a good king, they whetted the appetite for Christ. If they were a bad king (and most of them were bad!), they made the people long all the more for the real thing.

The promise of a king came early in the Bible (right back in Genesis), but its fulfilment was centuries in coming. Moses was not a 'king' *per se* and neither was Joshua. After Joshua there came a time of 'judges' (see the book of Judges). These were temporary rulers who delivered Israel from certain troubles. But still no 'king'.

Then we arrive in the book of 1 Samuel and the people clamour for a king, just like all the surrounding nations have (see 1 Sam. 8). But there's a surprise. The Lord relents and gives Israel their first king, but he's not from the royal tribe of Judah. His name is Saul and his reign is marked by cowardice and unbelief (1 Sam. 8–15). It's very much like the history of humanity's first ruler. Back in Genesis, the first king, Adam, was a failure, leading the people down the wrong path. What we needed was another king—a true ruler, Christ.

In 1 Samuel, the part of the true ruler is played by David. Once Saul has proven a total failure, God sends the prophet Samuel to a family from the tribe of Judah. Samuel tells Jesse, the father, that one of his eight sons will be king.

In 1 Samuel 16, seven strapping lads pass before Samuel, but none of them seem to be the Lord's choice. Finally Jesse's youngest appears, David. He's the one! The shepherd-boy! He is made king in a secret ceremony and the Holy Spirit fills him for the job.

So as we come to 'David and Goliath' (1 Sam. 17), this is the scene: The nation at large still thinks of Saul as king. But Saul is a failed and rejected king, leading the nation into shame and defeat. In reality, David is God's choice. The true king is the secret king. He is the weak-looking king. But he is God's king. And when he steps forward against Goliath, he shows what a true king does.

## THE PEOPLE'S CHAMPION

Here's the battle scene (read it all for yourself in 1 Sam. 17). Israel's army draws up its lines opposite the Philistines. They face off across the Valley of Elah and Goliath proposes a way of breaking the stalemate. He offers himself as the Philistines' Champion. He will fight a single Israelite opponent to the death. Winner takes all:

> Choose a man and have him come down to me. If he is able to fight and kill me, we will become your subjects; but if I overcome him and kill him, you will become our subjects and serve us... This day I

defy the ranks of Israel! Give me a man and let us
fight each other. (1 Sam. 17:8-10)

Goliath proposes this duel for 40 days. There are no
takers. Perhaps this is understandable. Goliath was a
giant of a man—a warrior from his youth. He wore
impressive scale armour, which reminds us of the
ancient serpent of Genesis 3. He was an apparently
super-natural enemy of God's people, accusing and
taunting them, day and night.

At this point, the reader should be asking
themselves: 'How will *Saul* respond to this?' Saul
should be leading the people in a spirited counter-
attack. But instead, he leads them in fear and shame:

> On hearing the Philistine's words, Saul and all the
> Israelites were dismayed and terrified. (1 Sam. 17:11)

This is such a dreadful indictment on Saul since he
was the natural choice to take on Goliath. He was 'a
head taller' than all the Israelites (1 Sam. 9:2). Saul
was Israel's giant. But he was also a coward. Here was
a failed king—one who would not lay down his life
for his people.

Step forward David, the true king, the secret king.
He wasn't even meant to be there. He was too young
for battle. He only came to bring supplies to his
brothers. This was not David's fight. But he made it
his fight when he heard the taunts of Goliath.

Incensed by the Philistine's goading, David
volunteers himself as Champion. His brothers think
he's arrogant. Saul thinks he's misguided. But David

persists and Saul allows a teenager to fight his battle for him.

So then, David and Goliath face off—champion against champion. Goliath wore a bronze helmet and scale armour. Just his coat of armour would have weighed more than David. He was also armed with a javelin, a spear and a shield.

David would have come up to Goliath's chest, if that. He wore no armour and his only weapon was a shepherd's slingshot.

Picture the faces of the soldiers who lined up behind these champions. What were the Philistines thinking? What were the Israelites thinking?

Well, in a sense, it doesn't matter. It doesn't matter what the armies were thinking. It doesn't matter what the armies were doing. It doesn't matter what the armies *could* do. It only matters what the champions do.

There are only two fighters here—everyone else is a spectator. The rank-and-file soldiers can do nothing to affect the end result. It would not help the champions in the slightest if, behind them, there was an army of motivated go-getters. It would not hinder them in the slightest if their compatriots were a despondent mass of no-hopers. The Israelite army could have its own cheerleading squad, shouting the most inspiring chants known to man. Or they could be asleep. It doesn't matter. The outcome of this battle has nothing to do with Israel's strength, or nerve, or willingness or faithfulness. All that matters is the victory of their champion. If their champion wins, the whole *nation* wins.

And then this happens:

> As the Philistine moved closer to attack him, David ran quickly towards the battle line to meet him. Reaching into his bag and taking out a stone, he slung it and struck the Philistine on the forehead. The stone sank into his forehead, and he fell face down on the ground. (1 Sam. 17:48-49)

David takes the Philistine's own weapon and finishes the job. Goliath is dead, Israel has the victory.

*Now* picture the faces of the soldiers. What a turnaround! The Philistines flee, the Israelites 'surge forwards with a shout' (v. 52). They have won the day. How? *Only* through the victory of their Champion.

## HIS VICTORY IS OUR VICTORY

This was David's first act as king. His first accomplishment is to defeat the people's enemy, bringing them freedom and joy. That's what a true 'King of the Jews' does. He stands up for his brothers—even when they doubt and disparage his motives. He fights for his people—even when they are too feeble and cowardly to fight for themselves. Through weakness and vulnerability he wins the day. And though his people have done nothing to contribute, his victory is their victory.

David shows us what the ultimate King of the Jews is like. When Jesus was born into our world, he came to a fight which was not his own. He did not have to join the battle against Satan. He could have left us to our terrifying adversary. He could have left us to the powers of sin and Satan, death and hell. But instead he volunteered himself as Champion.

He took our side, stepped into our shoes and stuck up for us in the only fight that really matters. As you picture the cross, you are picturing the ultimate David, walking out to battle against the ultimate Goliath, and he's doing it for you.

We cannot take on the powers that stand against the human race. Sin, death, judgement and Satan are much bigger than we are. But Jesus takes our side and fights for us.

Just before he died, Jesus spoke of Satan's defeat in these words:

Now the prince of this world will be driven out. (John 12:31)

The cross was the victory of Jesus. Everyone thought it would be the *end* of Jesus. Instead he made it a weapon *against* the devil. By it, he paid for sin, exhausted the judgement of death and hell, and conquered Satan. Through his death, Jesus wins the victory.

And who are we in this scene?

We are like the scared and feeble soldiers lined up behind their King. We have no hope against the Enemy. But Christ's victory is our victory.

## LOOKING TO THE KING

Imagine you were an Israelite soldier on the day David defeated Goliath. And imagine that next to you there

106

was a fellow-Israelite looking glum and disheartened. What would be the problem?

They must not have *seen* David's victory. Or if they have, they mustn't know their connection to David, their Champion. But if they *see* the victory and *know* their connection, they will shout for joy and move forwards in confidence.

It's the same with us. How do we find freedom and joy in life? Sometimes we think that we can take on life's challenges in our own strength. If so, we have no idea of the size of Goliath! Sometimes we despair that life is too much. Well, life *is* too much for us. But it's not too much for our Champion.

As we look to him, we see a victory that includes even us. We haven't expended a calorie of effort, and yet Christ, our Brother, has fought for us. Think of his courage, his grace, his strength and his love. He, the King, laid down his life for us. When that truth sinks in, *then* we will shout for joy, *then* we will move forwards in confidence and peace. And we will forever praise our Champion King!

*Keep reading...*

> 1 Samuel 17:1-58
> 1 Chronicles 17:1-27
> Psalm 72:1-20

*Keep thinking...*

What do you think is 'the moral' of the David and Goliath story?

Do you see the links between the following: the Israelites and us; Saul and Adam; Goliath and Satan; David and Christ? How does this story cast light on Jesus and what he's done?

How do you feel about your Champion winning the victory for you?

# Catch Up 2:
# Words of the Wise

Sitting in the middle of the Bible are five books that stand out from the rest. Sometimes they are called 'Wisdom Literature' because they are full of riddles and rhymes that need to be mulled over. These books came at different points in Israel's history but they are united by their kind of writing.

They are not histories—telling the stories of Israel. They are not prophecies—declaring God's word to a particular people in a particular situation. Instead they are songs and sayings, reflections and allegories that need to be chewed over and slowly digested. Yet all of them speak powerfully of Christ.

## JOB

This is an epic poem on the theme of suffering. It is the oldest biblical book to be written down. Job was a rough contemporary of Abraham.

He begins life in a wooded place in the East (like Eden). But through Satan there is a tragic fall and suffering devastates Job's world. Most of the book describes his wrestling with the horror of suffering. But in the end, Job is vindicated and restored to a greater glory than he ever enjoyed in the beginning.

Job's story is the story of humanity. We began in peace, fell into chaos but, through Christ—the truly righteous sufferer—humanity is raised to a happy ending, higher than ever.

PSALMS

This is Israel's hymn-book. Here we find 150 songs—many of them written by King David. They are songs of joy and sorrow, of love and war, of hope and desperation. The first two Psalms introduce us to the four main characters of the book:

1. The Lord / The Father

2. The King / The Christ / The Upright Man / God's Son

3. The wicked (those who oppose Christ)

4. The righteous (those who take refuge in Christ)

Virtually all the Psalms unfold an interaction between these four characters. Some Psalms are prayers of the Upright Man (Christ) to the Lord (the Father). Some are cries from the righteous to be protected from the wicked. Some are the words of the Lord to pay heed to Christ. But all of them reveal Jesus in their various ways.

## PROVERBS

This book also involves four main characters:

1. The King

2. His son

3. Wisdom

4. Folly

Essentially the book is a fire-side chat between the King and his son, the crown prince. The father's advice boils down to this: 'Watch out for the ladies!' There's a wonderful woman called 'Wisdom' and a real *femme fatale* called 'Folly'. Success in life depends on getting Wisdom and shunning Folly.

But who *are* these women? As the book unfolds it becomes clear that Folly is a satanic figure and Wisdom is incredibly Christ-like. Wisdom was there in the beginning, creating the universe at the Lord's side and giving us the grace of God (see Prov. 8–9). Thus 'being wise' is not so much about making the right decisions. It's about being united to the right Person. Right living (Prov. 10–31) flows out of a relationship with Christ (Prov. 1–9).

## ECCLESIASTES

Here is the spiritual journal of 'the son of David, king of Jerusalem' (Eccles. 1:1).

But if we were hoping for some royal encouragement, we'll be royally disappointed. *This* king declares all life 'meaningless', it's 'miserable business', it's 'a chasing after the wind'.

How can he be so bleak? Well, the book is written from the perspective of 'life under the sun'. In other words, he's thinking about life in the here and now, where God does not break in to save. He merely sits above us to judge. It's a life where our only hope is our own work and wit. But, ultimately, it's futile because the grave swallows us all.

Ecclesiastes is an unrelenting look at life through the lens of our own mortality. And it makes us cry out for another 'Son of David'—for another 'King of the Jews'. We need Jesus to break into our world, to be our Saviour and to defeat death. Only then will we have an answer to meaninglessness.

## SONG OF SONGS

Here is a beautiful love poem in which a young couple—the lover and the beloved—sing to each other. At the same time there is a deeper meaning.

The lover is often spoken of as being like the Lord and the beloved is described in ways reminiscent of God's people. This makes sense when you consider the Bible's descriptions of the Lord and his people. Many times, Christ calls himself a husband or a bridegroom. Often, the people are known as his bride.

So in Song of Songs we have, not only a story of human love, but a celebration of the kind of love Christ has for us. He doesn't merely rule us as the ultimate Master; he loves us as our ultimate Spouse. And just like in a marriage, we can say to Jesus: 'My lover is mine and I am his' (Song. 2:16).

# 9
# Getting Carried Away

These days, 'getting carried away' is not so serious. Perhaps we're overcome by a bout of silliness. Or we lose track of the time in conversation. Or we go a bit far as we rant about some pet topic.

But, in the Bible, to be 'carried away' was devastating. The phrase comes to us from older translations of the Bible. It describes God's people, forcibly removed from their homeland, and dragged into exile.

> Israel [was] carried away out of their own land. (2 Kings 17:23, KJV)

Have you ever been wrenched from your home? What does it feel like?

## HOMESICK
The Bible describes being carried away in a number of ways. It's like being 'uprooted' (e.g. Deut. 28:63). Picture a plant, torn out of its soil, roots dangling

in mid-air, tossed across the field and left there, disconnected. It is no longer grounded in the place it knows. That's one description.

Another description is being 'a stranger in a strange land' (Exod. 2:22, KJV). You are strange to the new place and it is strange to you. You're like a 'fly in the ointment' (Eccles. 10:1) and neither you nor your new home are happy about the situation!

Another way of saying 'carried away' is to say 'uncovered'. The Bible's word for 'carried away' conjures up images of being stripped bare. When we're not at home, we can feel exposed, vulnerable and naked.

Do you relate to these descriptions of home-sickness?

Actually, the Bible says that we are all homesick. We are all, to an extent, restless and estranged. We might never have left the place of our birth, but there's a deeper sense in which we're 'not at home'.

Ever since the Garden of Eden we've been exiled from our natural habitat. We should be at home with God. Instead we are, to some degree, 'rootless', 'strangers' and 'uncovered'.

When the Israelites were exiled from their land it was a physical manifestation of a spiritual truth. We desperately want to be home. But instead we live 'East of Eden', and until this spiritual exile is ended, we will all be restless wanderers.

## THE KINGDOM: DIVIDED
## AND CONQUERED

Last chapter we met David—the first of the Judah-ite kings. As 'king of the Jews' he was meant to picture Christ to the people. He reigned on mount Zion in Jerusalem and everything he did was meant to picture something of eternal and global significance. He performed many Christ-like acts—like when he defeated Goliath on behalf of the people. But in other ways he failed spectacularly—like when he got his friend's wife pregnant and then ordered the friend's death to cover it up (2 Sam. 11–12). This was the way with the kings of Judah. At best they were mixed representatives of Christ.

Next after David came his son: wise king Solomon. Again, Solomon provided some early glimpses of the righteous rule of Christ (1 Kings 2–10; cf. Ps. 45, 72). But, once more, his later years were a major disappointment (1 Kings 11).

After Solomon, the kingdom split between the north and the south (1 Kings 12). The north kept the name 'Israel' for themselves. The south called themselves 'Judah' and they maintained the promised royal line.

There were twenty northern kings after Solomon. The Scriptures judge that all of them 'did not do what was right in the eyes of the LORD'. There were twenty southern kings after Solomon. The Scriptures judge that eight of them 'did what was right'; the rest did not.

All in all, there was a relentless decline from the time of Solomon. God's people descended into greater and greater wickedness. Eventually both north and south were judged by the Lord. Just as Israel had judged the Canaanites for their evils, so Israel was judged by foreign armies.

First 'Israel' was defeated and 'carried away' by the Assyrian super-power (2 Kings 17). Later, 'Judah' was 'carried away' by the Babylonian super-power (2 Kings 24–25). This means its people were put to the sword, with the survivors shackled and taken far away to be slaves.

While Judah was enslaved in Babylon the people sang their lament, made famous by Boney-M:

> By the rivers of Babylon we sat and wept when we remembered Zion. (Ps. 137:1)

Singing was one response to these events. Another response was to speak into these crises. That was the job of the prophets and they played a major role in Israel's history before and after exile.

## THE PROPHETS

The word prophet means 'One who speaks before'. This definition contains a double meaning. Does the 'before' refer to a location or a timeframe? Are they speaking before an audience or before a future event? Are they forth-tellers or fore-tellers? Are they preaching about today or predicting tomorrow? Really the answer is Yes. The prophets brought a blistering critique of Israel's present while simultaneously painting a dazzling portrait of God's future.

In your Bible the bulk of the prophets are found as the last seventeen books of the Old Testament. First there are the major prophets: Isaiah, Jeremiah and Ezekiel. In amongst these major prophets are Lamentations and Daniel (these books are not as long). Then there are the twelve minor prophets ('minor' simply in terms of length).

Some prophets spoke from the northern kingdom ('Israel'); some from the southern kingdom ('Judah'). Some spoke before the exile, some during and some after, but all of them had this dual focus of revealing the people's sinfulness and the Lord's salvation.

A brief survey of the prophet Isaiah will give a sense of how they did this.

Isaiah was from the southern kingdom of Judah and while mourning the death of good king Uzziah (one of the few good kings), he met with the great I AM in the temple:

> In the year that King Uzziah died, I saw the LORD, seated on a throne, high and exalted, and the train of his robe filled the temple. (Isa. 6:1)

If you search online for images of 'divine encounters' you will find lots of soft focus, warm light, arms outstretched in liberation and joy. That's not how it is in the Bible. When people meet God in the Bible they are flattened by his uncreated glory. Isaiah cries out in terror!

'Woe to me!' I cried. 'I am ruined! For I am a man of unclean lips, and I live among a people of unclean lips, and my eyes have seen the King, the LORD Almighty.' (Isa. 6:5)

The appearance of the Lord is like an asteroid crashing down into Isaiah's world. He is ruined and cries 'Woe is me'. That's where a true encounter with God leaves us: unable to point the finger at anyone else but profoundly aware of our own spiritual poverty.

The Lord does not keep Isaiah on his face though. The pattern is always that people are driven down before the Lord, *then* raised up (1 Pet. 5:6). Isaiah is no different. The Lord makes forgiveness fly to Isaiah (verses 6-7), then he is set on his feet to preach to the nation. And what will be Isaiah's message?

## THUS SAITH THE LORD

The message of Isaiah is typical of the message of all the prophets. He preaches utter doom and jaw-dropping hope. In Isaiah 6, the message he is given to proclaim is this: Israel is a tree about to be felled. The axe is at the root and the whole thing is coming down. All the prophets preach like this. They tell the people: *Judgement is coming and there's no escape. You will be carried away into exile.* And it doesn't matter if the people promise to be good from now on, it doesn't matter if they perform all the rituals and keep all the festivals, it doesn't matter if they have the temple and all the trappings of religion, they are getting the chop. Israel's only hope is on the far side of judgement. From beyond exile the Messiah will come.

Isaiah is told:

> But as the terebinth and oak
>> leave stumps when they are cut down,
> so the holy seed will be the stump. (Isa. 6:13)

The people are the tree. The Babylonian superpower is the lumberjack. Who is the holy seed that brings new life once the tree is chopped down? Perhaps it helps to know that the word 'seed' is the same as the word 'offspring'. It's Christ. On the far side of exile, Christ will spring up and bring fresh hope for Israel and the whole world.

Isaiah 11 puts it like this:

> A shoot will come up from the stump of Jesse;[1]
>> from his roots a Branch will bear fruit.
> The Spirit of the LORD will rest on him—
>> the Spirit of wisdom and of understanding,
> the Spirit of counsel and of power,
>> the Spirit of the knowledge and of the fear of
> the LORD. (Isa. 11:1-3)

> In that day the Root of Jesse will stand as a banner for the peoples; the nations will rally to him, and his place of rest will be glorious. (Isa. 11:10)

This is the message of all the prophets. The end is nigh for the nation-state of Israel. They are being judged for their sins and their hope is not in their goodness, their rituals, their history, their armies,

---

1. Jesse was David's father.

their buildings or their ethnic identity. Their hope is in their Messiah—the Seed, the Offspring of David, the true Spirit-filled King.

The prophets all spoke like this. On one hand they declare our hopeless condition in ourselves; then they herald our incredible hope in God. Putting ourselves in the sandals of an Israelite we are given a two-fold experience. We hear the prophet thunder his critique of our darkness and inadequacy. But then we hold on, trusting not to our goodness but only to Christ, and as we do so we hear heart-stopping promises:

On this mountain the Lord Almighty will prepare
    a feast of rich food for all peoples,
a banquet of aged wine—
    the best of meats and the finest of wines.
On this mountain he will destroy
    the shroud that enfolds all peoples,
the sheet that covers all nations;
    he will swallow up death for ever.
The Sovereign Lord will wipe away the tears
    from all faces;
he will remove the disgrace of his people
    from all the earth.
The Lord has spoken.

In that day they will say,

'Surely this is our God;
    we trusted in him, and he saved us.
This is the Lord, we trusted in him;
    let us rejoice and be glad in his salvation.'
(Isa. 25:6-9)

When we hear the prophets in their two-fold ministry, it strips away our *self*-confidence but leaves us with something far more secure: Christ-confidence. Beyond all our failure he will bring us home to a future of feasting joy.

## RETURN FROM EXILE?

It was 722 BC when the northern kingdom was 'carried away' into exile. They never recovered. They were uprooted and scattered, never to be gathered again. The southern kingdom was 'carried away' in 587 BC. Judah was first enslaved by the Babylonians but then Babylon was overthrown by the Medes and Persians. After seventy years of captivity, the Persian king, Cyrus, allowed the Jews to return to Jerusalem. At that time there was a physical resettlement in the land (you can read about this in books like Ezra and Nehemiah). But this was not a real homecoming.

It would take more than a building project to end Israel's spiritual estrangement. You can have the right postal code but that doesn't mean you're at home with God. No, it's *Jesus* who truly ends the exile.

That's almost the first thing which the New Testament teaches. In the first chapter of Matthew, the first of the four Gospels, we gain a bird's-eye view of Israelite history. Matthew mentions three key historical moments prior to Christ's coming: Abraham, David and the exile. Notice how Matthew says the exile ends:

Thus there were fourteen generations in all from Abraham to David, fourteen from David to the exile to Babylon, and fourteen from the exile to the Christ. (Matt. 1:17)

The end of exile is not some ancient rehousing scheme. Jesus is the end of exile. He brings the presence of God to earth.

## TRUE HOMECOMING

Without the New Testament the Old Testament would be profoundly dissatisfying. Having begun with cosmic themes in Genesis, it ends in Malachi with a tiny remnant of the southern portion of a downtrodden people. They have been chewed up and spat out by just about every major power on the world stage and now they huddle together around a rebuilt temple that is a shadow of its former glory (Ezra 3:12; Hag. 2:3). Really all they have is their Messianic hope. In themselves they have nothing, but Israel was never about focusing attention on itself.

Everything about the Old Testament points beyond itself. The law, the tabernacle, the sacrifices, the priests, the battles, the kings, the land—these were all signs of a deeper spiritual reality. None of these Old Testament shadows provided spiritual sustenance themselves. They all consciously pointed forwards to a future fulfilment.

*Christ* is the true fulfilment of the law—the Son of God who perfectly lives the Good Life.

*Christ* is the true tabernacle—the meeting place of God and man.

*Christ* is the true sacrifice—the Lamb of God who takes away the sin of the world.

*Christ* is the true priest—the Go-Between who carries us to God.

*Christ* is the true Joshua—bringing us into God's promised rest.

*Christ* is the true king—the righteous Ruler who fights for our freedom.

And *Christ* is the true land—the dwelling place of God who invites us home.

If we consider the Old Testament without Christ we are reading a tragedy—a particularly cruel one too, given the hopes it continually holds out. But if we let the Old Testament proclaim its Messianic hope then we realise the story is far from over. Really the first thirty-nine books have set the scene. Now—if we identify with scattered Israel, if we too feel rootless and dislocated—we are ready for Christ to enter into our estrangement. We are ready to see the promised King drawing near and making his dwelling among us. If we have read the Old Testament rightly, now as we turn the page to the New, it will feel like coming home.

*Keep reading…*

2 Chronicles 36:1-23
Isaiah 6
Isaiah 11

*Keep thinking…*

Do you agree that humanity suffers from homesickness? What would it be like to truly come home?

The prophets speak devastating home truths about our sin yet also promise wonderful blessings for our future. Which do you find easier to believe? How could both be true?

Do you see the way that Jesus fulfils the Old Testament shadows of law, sacrificial system, kings and land?

# Catch Up 3:
# The Prophets and the Return[1]

|  | To Israel | To Judah | To Foreign Nations |
|---|---|---|---|
| Assyrian Age | Amos (c. 763-750 BC) Hosea (c. 755-715 BC) | Isaiah (c. 740-770 BC) Micah (c. 737-690 BC) | Jonah (c. 770-750 BC) |
| Babylo-nian Age |  | Habakkuk (c. 630-605 BC) Zephaniah (c. 640-609 BC) Jeremiah (c. 627-580 BC) Daniel (c. 605-530 BC) Ezekiel (c. 593-570 B.C) | Nahum (c. 663-615 BC) |

---

1. Based on table from *Archaeological Study Bible* (Grand Rapids, MI: Zondervan, 2005), p. 1483.

| | | Haggai<br>(520 BC)<br><br>Zechariah<br>(c. 520-518 BC)<br><br>Joel<br>(c. 800-500 BC)<br><br>Malachi<br>(c. 433 BC) | Obadiah<br>(c. 586-553 BC) |
|---|---|---|---|
| Persian<br>Age | | | |

# 10

# The Heavens Opened

When we speak of the heavens opening it usually means rain: 'We got through seventeen holes of golf alright but then *the heavens opened.*' In our conversations, 'the heavens opened' is shorthand for a torrential downpour.

In the Bible, the phrase is used more literally. There was an occasion when the heavens were in fact torn open and we got to see inside. I wonder what you imagine was there. What does it look like to see ultimate spiritual reality? When the curtain is drawn back, what is God really like? The Gospels show us.

## GOOD NEWS!

The New Testament begins with four biographies of Jesus: Matthew, Mark, Luke and John. Each are called 'Gospels'. The word 'gospel' in Greek is the word 'evangel' and it means 'good news'. To 'evange*lise*' means to announce good news, to proclaim gospel truth. It means declaring that something earth-shatteringly wonderful has happened. If your New Testament begins with the heading, 'The Gospel According to Matthew', what it's really saying is 'The astonishingly brilliant news that changes everything for everyone, as told by Matthew'. That's the meaning of 'Gospel'.

Imagine you are an Israelite lining up behind David as he faces off against Goliath. You just can't watch the fight because you know that Goliath is about to tear the poor boy limb from limb. You're staring at your sandals waiting for it all to be over and suddenly a teller of good news gets up, an evangelist. 'LOOK!' he bellows. 'David has triumphed! Goliath is dead. Victory is ours!' That's the announcement of good news that changes everything. It's what the Gospels are all about.

Matthew, Mark, Luke and John are evangelists. Matthew and John were part of Jesus' closest band of followers—the twelve disciples. Mark was recording the remembrances of Peter—the chief disciple. Luke was an historian working from eye-witness accounts. All of them were declaring good news. They proclaimed that our true David has come. He might look weak and hopeless, but He's actually the Spirit-filled Son of God. He's our true King, our Champion. And *Look!* He has won the victory over sin, death, hell and Satan. 'Death is dead, love has won, Christ has conquered', as the song says. That is the message of the Gospels.

## BEGINNING AGAIN WITH JESUS

John's Gospel is the most translated and most widely-distributed of the Gospels. As such it is one of the most read pieces of literature in human history. It opens with an epic introduction, reminiscent of the Bible's first verse:

> In the beginning was the Word, and the Word was with God, and the Word was God. (John 1:1)

To paint a portrait of Christ, John thinks we ought to use a cosmic canvas. As John pens Jesus' biography he goes back before the world began. In doing so he affirms what we were exploring in chapter 1 of this book: the Son of God is older than the universe. Before anything else existed there was a Father loving his Son in the joy of the Spirit. John is telling us that *Jesus* is that 'Son'. Here, though, John uses a different title for him: 'the Word'. What does it mean that Jesus is 'the Word'?

It means that Jesus is the expression of God, the communication of God. He's everything God wants to say to the world, wrapped up in a person. If we want to know God, Jesus explains him perfectly. Everything we hear Jesus saying and everything we see Jesus doing reveals God the Father.

Imagine a comic trying to depict heaven. You can't see much because of the dazzling glory. There's a figure on the throne but you can't see him. All you can see is a giant speech bubble coming out from the throne. What's inside the speech bubble? Jesus. He *is* God's Word to the world. Jesus reveals the heart and soul, the name and nature of the living God. And he has always done so. What we read in the Gospels is how this 'Word' came among us to reveal God's true nature. If we keep reading John we will see Jesus drawing near, loving, healing, touching, teaching, suffering, bleeding and dying for us. That's what God is like. God is like Jesus.

## THE CHRIST-LIKE GOD

Tom Torrance was an army chaplain in World War II. In October 1944 he was acting as a stretcher-bearer in Italy. He came across a young soldier named Private Phillips, barely 20 years old. It was clear that the soldier was bleeding out from his wounds and would soon die. The private saw that Torrance was a chaplain—a padre—and asked, 'Padre, is God really like Jesus?'

That's the question a man asks when he's about to meet his Maker. When everything else is stripped away, this is a question of eternal significance: Is God like Jesus? Can we trust him?

Torrance assured the man that God is entirely and utterly like Jesus, because Jesus *is* the very Word of God. The God revealed by Jesus is the only God there is. He has come down to us, showed his face to us, and poured out his love for us as Saviour. What we see in Jesus is what we get with God. Always.

Torrance prayed for the man and entrusted him to the keeping of *this* God, the Christ-like God. As he prayed, the soldier died. For us the question remains alive: Is God really like Jesus? Do we entrust ourselves to *this* kind of God? The Gospels tell us that when we see Jesus in all his towering charisma and stooping love, we are seeing the true God.

This is wonderful news. But there is more. In seeing Jesus we don't just see true deity. We also see true humanity.

## THE WORD BECAME FLESH
John's Gospel goes on to say:

> The Word became flesh and made his dwelling among us. (John 1:14)

It's the ultimate Christmas text, read at every carol service all over the world. But perhaps we miss the immensity of it. 'The Word' is the creator of heaven and earth. On the other hand, 'flesh' is a shocking word to use.

In the old Latin translations you would read the word 'carnis'. It's the source of the word 'incarnation'. It's also the origin of *chilli con carne*. What is *chilli con carne*? It's *chilli with meat!* That's the sense of the word 'flesh' here. The Word became *meat*.

Ask a biologist to describe humanity and they might use the phrase '*homo sapiens*'. Ask a philosopher to describe humanity and they might say 'a rational animal'. Ask a butcher to describe humanity and they might say 'carnis', 'flesh', meat!

When Jesus finally came in the New Testament it was not a heavenly visitation. It was not like those temporary appearances in the Old Testament to

Moses or Isaiah. In the Old Testament, the Word was not in any sense anchored to earth. He was not one of us. He came and went. It was all so shadowy. But in the New Testament the Word earths himself into our humanity for all time.

As we read the Gospels we realise that Jesus was a real man: growing, learning, hungering, thirsting, tiring, sleeping. He did not float six inches off the ground. He did not have a constant halo around him. The Word did not descend like a deep-sea diver, wearing a man-suit. The Word did not 'put on' flesh; the Word did not 'enter' flesh; the Word did not 'borrow' some flesh or 'hide behind' flesh or 'get diluted' in flesh. No, the Word *became* flesh: flesh that had to be slapped to elicit that precious first breath; flesh that got nappy rash; flesh that got acne; flesh that got sunburnt in the Mediterranean heat; flesh that could be bruised; flesh that could be cut; flesh that could bleed. The Word entered into our humanity fully and forever.

If someone has been particularly callous, we might ask them: 'Where's your humanity?' We use such language because we reckon that 'having humanity' will mean having a heart, having sympathy. Let's then ask ourselves about God: 'Where's God's humanity?' Does he have a heart? Does he have sympathy? The Gospels say, Absolutely. Since Christmas God now has humanity. Forevermore God will be the humanitarian God. He has taken up our cause to be our champion.

## CHAMPION

When Jesus was 30 he left behind the family business, carpentry, and went public with his heavenly mission. He did this at a ceremony that looked just like David's coronation back in the Old Testament. In 1 Samuel 16, David was anointed with oil (a symbol of the Holy Spirit) to mark him out as king. Straight afterwards David took on Goliath, a superhuman enemy of God's people (1 Sam. 17). In Matthew chapter 3, Jesus is baptised (i.e. given a ritual wash) and the Holy Spirit publicly comes upon him. Straight afterwards he takes on Satan, the superhuman enemy of God's people (Matt. 4). The message was clear: Jesus is the true David and he has come to fight for us. It happened this way:

> Then Jesus came from Galilee to the Jordan to be baptised by John [the Baptist]. But John tried to deter him, saying, 'I need to be baptised by you, and do you come to me?' (Matt. 3:13-14)

'John the Baptist' is not the same 'John' as the author of John's Gospel. John the Baptist was actually Jesus' cousin. He is conducting the baptisms—that is, he is giving people a ritual wash in the Jordan River. It was explicitly a ceremony for *sinners*, for those who know they need an inner cleansing. But then Jesus joins the queue. John is baffled. Why on earth would the perfect, pure Son of God need to take a bath? Jesus is the one person who *doesn't* need baptism. So what's going on?

> Jesus replied, 'Let it be so now; it is proper for us to do this to fulfil all righteousness.' Then John consented. (Matt. 3:15)

Jesus says 'Let's do it this way around'. Why? Because this is the whole reason he 'became flesh'. He is entering *our* mess. Jesus is our David, volunteering for a fight that is not his. He is joining us in our humanity and shouldering all our burdens. He's like a star footballer signing for a failing club. The baptism is like the photo call with all the journalists. He is publicly wearing the colours of his new team and now he identifies with these losers in full. From now on he will own them and they will own him. Every goal he scores, he scores for the team. He will be their champion.

This is good news, but what does it mean for his relationship with God the Father and with the Spirit? As Jesus associates with sinners on earth, will heaven disassociate from him? No, the very opposite:

> As soon as Jesus was baptised, he went up out of the water. At that moment **heaven was opened**, and he saw the Spirit of God descending like a dove and lighting on him. And a voice from heaven said, 'This is my Son, whom I love; with him I am well pleased.' (Matt. 3:16-17)

When Jesus joins our family that does *not* mean he's out of God's family. No, Jesus is emphatically declared to be the beloved Son of God, even as he openly unites himself to filthy sinners like us. You might imagine that the Father and Spirit would distance themselves from Jesus now that he is rubbing shoulders with 'the wrong crowd'. On the contrary, God wants the world to know that Jesus is expressing his own good pleasure and love.

*This* is what we see when the heavens are opened. Not storm clouds. And not a stormy God either. The God *Jesus* reveals is a Father brimming with love and joy, a God who generously pours out his Spirit on a Son who pours himself out for the world. When the heavens are opened we see not rain but *love* overflowing.

## WHAT TO EXPECT IN THE GOSPELS

The baptism was the launch of Jesus' public ministry. From that moment onwards, Jesus champions our cause, taking up our fight. He goes immediately into the wilderness to face off with the devil. This is round one of his fight with Satan and it sets the scene for the rest of the Gospels. Throughout them we read how Jesus takes on our enemies for us. Temptation, sickness, the forces of nature, the powers of evil— these get the better of us. Yet Jesus, our Champion, conquers them. At the end of the Gospels Jesus takes on the big four: Satan, sin, judgement and death. The Gospels major on the Easter events because that is where he really defeats these enemies.

Jesus' cross and resurrection fulfils everything the Bible proclaims. There Jesus showed himself to be:

The true *Offspring* (or 'Seed'), going down into the ground and springing up to new life.

The true *Isaac*, the beloved Son offered on the mountain but received back alive.

The true *burning bush*, the great I AM who enters our furnace to secure our redemption.

The true *Passover Lamb*, slain in our place to deliver us from judgement.

The true *Joshua*, fighting through the wilderness of death to bring us to his promised hope.

The true *David*, taking on our Enemy and gaining the victory.

The true *Israel*, cursed and alienated then raised to a glorious homecoming.

Across the top of all four Gospels you could write two simple words: 'for us'. Jesus is the God who takes our side, shoulders our burdens, engages our foes, dies our death and brings us victory. How then should we read the Gospels?

Martin Luther, the sixteenth-century church reformer, wrote a short booklet entitled 'What to Look for and Expect in the Gospels.' His chief piece of advice was this: 'Before you take Christ as an example... accept and recognise him as a gift.' Jesus *is* a moral example for us, that is true. But that's not the primary thing to take from the Gospels. First we must see that he is a gift—a gift given to those who fail to copy Jesus. Jesus has been given as our Champion, to live our life for us and die our death for us. This is the fundamental truth to grasp from the Gospels. The Evangelists—Matthew, Mark, Luke and John—are not, basically, drill sergeants yelling at you, urging you to copy your King. '*See how David beat Goliath, now you have a go!*'

Essentially the Gospels are heralds of Christ, telling you 'Look! He's done it! You can move forwards, you have the victory!'

Now *that's* good news.

*Keep reading...*

John 1:1-18
Matthew 3:13–4:25
John 19:1–20:18

*Keep thinking...*

Do you often imagine God to be un-Christ-like? What kind of God does *Jesus* reveal?

What difference does it make that Christ 'became flesh'? Why did he do it?

What's the difference between reading the Gospels like they are drill sergeants and reading them like they are heralds of victory? How might seeing them as heralds change your reading of the Bible? How might it change *you*?

# 11

# Damascus Road

It's shorthand for a dramatic conversion. If someone undergoes a shocking turnaround, we might say they've had a Damascus Road Experience. We use the expression in all kinds of contexts, whether religious or not. An artist might 'see the light' and realise their work needs to go in a wholly new direction. A politician might speak of 'the scales falling from their eyes' when they realise they need to make a U-turn (Acts 9:18). A health-food guru might have 'a Damascene experience' when they encounter the wonders of a new diet. People have often said to me, whether Christians or not, that they're still waiting for their 'Damascus Road Experience'.

All these people are referencing a famous event in the book of Acts. There the church's greatest enemy, Saul of Tarsus, was on his way to Damascus to further persecute the followers of Jesus. On the road, he had an encounter with Christ in which he was dramatically converted and became Paul—preacher, missionary, church-planter, and author of half the New Testament.

Understanding the Damascus Road will help us grasp Paul's biography, the unfolding of the Bible's story and the heart of Christianity itself. It might even help us have our own Damascene experience!

## ACTS

The Gospels climax with Easter and then the risen Jesus gives his people their marching orders. Having accomplished our salvation, Jesus calls his people to become 'evangelists'—that is, heralds of the good news (Matt. 28:16-20; Mark 16:9-20; Luke 24:36-53; John 20:19-23).

With Jesus returning to heaven, the book of Acts records what happened next. It was written by Luke, the Evangelist, as a follow-up to his Gospel. It tells of how the followers of Jesus 'turned the world upside down' (Acts 17:6, KJV).

The revolution began in Jerusalem, seven weeks after Easter. Jesus had promised that when he returned to heaven, he would pour out the Holy Spirit on his followers to equip them in a new and powerful way. He did this on a day called 'Pentecost'.

Pentecost was a major festival in the Jewish calendar and multitudes came to Jerusalem from all over the world. On this particular Pentecost the international visitors were astonished to hear the followers of Jesus preaching, each in their native tongue. The people demanded an explanation for this miracle.

Peter stood up to address the crowd knowing that they had last been assembled at the feast of Passover, seven weeks earlier. On that occasion the crowds had demanded Jesus' blood and witnessed his execution. Now Peter tells them:

> God has raised this Jesus to life, and we are all witnesses of the fact. Exalted to the right hand of God, he has received from the Father the promised Holy Spirit and has poured out what you now see and hear. (Acts 2:32-33)

He went on:

> Let all Israel be assured of this: God has made this Jesus, whom you crucified, both Lord and Messiah. (Acts 2:36, NIV 2011)

This is shocking news for the crowd. They had not only participated in the death of an innocent man. He was the *Lord*. They were meant to wait for and welcome the Messiah, instead they had killed him! How did they react?

> When the people heard this, they were cut to the heart and said to Peter and the other apostles, 'Brothers, what shall we do?'
>
> Peter replied, 'Repent and be baptised, every one of you, in the name of Jesus Christ for the forgiveness of your sins. And you will receive the gift of the Holy Spirit.' (Acts 2:38)

Here Peter plays the part of a prophet perfectly. He preaches doom, then hope. He cuts to the heart, then offers mercy. And what astonishing mercy it is. He tells people who had killed the Lord that God wants to forgive them, and not just forgive them but offer them a gift. And not just any gift, but the gift of the Holy Spirit.

The piling on of grace upon grace is incredible. God had given us his Son. We killed him. In response God says, 'I want to forgive you and offer another "family member", so to speak'. It was a case of: *You've killed my Son; here have my Spirit!* It would be like a Judge telling a condemned criminal that not only was he forgiven for killing his boy, the murderer could have his daughter's hand in marriage too. Astonishing!

Three thousand people responded to this message and were baptised. To understand baptism we just need to remember Christ's baptism from the previous chapter. It's all about solidarity: at Jesus' baptism he identified with us; in our baptism we identify with him. We stand in the waters with Jesus, as it were. We confess our sins and unworthiness but right there we find Christ identifying with us, we find the Father proclaiming his love over us, we find his Spirit filling us. Baptism is about a whole new life with Jesus at the centre and on the day of Pentecost thousands entered into that life.

A few days after Pentecost, Peter preaches again and 5000 believe. The revolution is well under way. It ripples from Jerusalem to the surrounding countryside and from there to neighbouring regions. As it does so, this new movement becomes profoundly threatening to the Jewish establishment. One man saw it as his God-given calling to end the disturbance once and for all.

## SAUL

By his own admission, Saul was extremely religious. He took pride in his race (Jewish), his tribe (Benjaminite), his schooling (Gamaliel's, i.e. the best), his moral law-keeping (flawless) and his religious sect (the very strictest, known as the 'Pharisees'). But despite this heritage (or perhaps because of it) Saul vehemently rejected the claims of Jesus. Saul was a ladder-climber. Jesus' movement went in the opposite direction. Jesus was a Messiah who stooped down to sinners. Saul, on the other hand, was a go-getter who lived for self-improvement. No wonder Saul found Jesus, at best, to be a distasteful candidate for Messiah. Yet it was worse than that. Surely it was blasphemous to imagine God on the cross. Surely God was a standard to aspire to, not a penniless preacher who chokes to death in shame. No, the Jesus movement could not be right and it certainly could not be tolerated.

In Acts 7, Saul gets his first taste of blood. Stephen, an early Christian leader, is stoned to death. Saul wasn't exactly the ring-leader. That was too messy a job for such a cultured man. Saul was in the background, enabling others to get blood on their hands (Acts 7:58; 8:1). Unfortunately for Saul though, killing Stephen was a little like killing Jesus—it only seemed to aid the cause. So as the movement grows, Saul finds himself having to stamp out Christianity well beyond Jerusalem:

143

Meanwhile, Saul was still breathing out murderous threats against the Lord's disciples. He went to the high priest and asked him for letters to the synagogues in Damascus, so that if he found any there who belonged to the Way [a name for the early Christians], whether men or women, he might take them as prisoners to Jerusalem. (Acts 9:1-3)

This was the context for the Damascus Road encounter. Saul was not at all looking for a Christian experience—the very opposite. But Jesus had other ideas.

As he neared Damascus on his journey, suddenly a light from heaven flashed around him. He fell to the ground and heard a voice say to him, 'Saul, Saul, why do you persecute me?'

'Who are you, Lord?' Saul asked.

'I am Jesus, whom you are persecuting,' he replied. 'Now get up and go into the city, and you will be told what you must do.' (Acts 9:3-6)

In this event the seeds for the rest of Saul's life are sown. From this moment on, Saul becomes Paul and is the central figure in the book of Acts. He is also the chief author of the rest of the Bible. He will go on to preach model sermons (Acts 13 and 17 in particular) and to write half the New Testament (the letters from Romans to Philemon).

In the end he would be persecuted for his teaching just as harshly as he had persecuted others. Tradition has it that Paul was beheaded for his Christian faith in Rome around AD 64. But everything he taught and all that he stood for traces back to the Damascus Road.

In this event Saul experienced a revolution in how he considered four realities: Jesus, salvation, the church, and its mission. Those four revolutions are reflected in all his teaching. We will explore them now in turn.

## JESUS IS LORD

The first revolution—the revolution from which all others spring—is to know Jesus as Lord. Previously, Saul had imagined that, whoever 'the Lord' was, he could have nothing to do with the shame and suffering of the Jesus story. Now, in an instant, Saul realises how wrong he was. Jesus *is* the Lord.

Paul proceeds to rethink his entire approach to faith and the Scriptures. In his preaching and writing he constantly shows how the Old Testament had in fact been preaching Jesus all along. As Paul stands on trial for his Christian proclamation, he declares:

> 'I am saying nothing beyond what the prophets and Moses said would happen—that the [Messiah] would suffer and, as the first to rise from the dead, proclaim light to his own people and to the [nations]' (Acts 26:22-23).

In other words, the Scriptures have always been about Christ: his death and resurrection. This is why the Christians called themselves 'the Way'. They were not a sect *departing* from the way of Moses or narrowing it. Christian faith was quite simply 'the Way'—the Way it has always been from Adam onwards. Jesus is Lord and has always been Lord.

## SALVATION IS GRACIOUS

If Jesus chose Saul, his greatest enemy, to become Paul, his greatest advocate, then salvation really must be *all* about mercy. The way of God cannot be the ladder-climbing religion which Saul had assumed it was. If it were then Saul would be swept aside as a rebel and God would choose some soft-hearted Jesus-lover to write the New Testament. But no, Paul is saved right in the midst of his murderous, Christ-hating frenzy.

Paul continually reflects on this in his writing. In his first letter to Timothy, his protégé, he says:

> Here is a trustworthy saying that deserves full acceptance: Christ Jesus came into the world to save sinners—of whom I am the worst. But for that very reason I was shown mercy so that in me, the worst of sinners, Christ Jesus might display his unlimited patience as an example for those who would believe on him and receive eternal life. (1 Tim. 1:15–16)

The whole world should look on Paul and say, 'If Jesus saved even *him,* anyone can be saved.' That's the heartbeat of Paul's letters. As he writes to the Ephesians: 'it is by grace you have been saved, through faith—and this not from yourselves, it is the gift of God—not by works, so that no one can boast' (Eph. 2:8-9).

## THE CHURCH IS CHRIST'S BODY

Jesus says something curious on the Damascus Road: 'Saul, Saul, why are you persecuting *me?*' This is odd. Saul wasn't persecuting *Jesus,* was he? He was only persecuting Jesus' followers. Except that Jesus took it *very* personally. He identifies with his people so closely that to harm the church is to harm Jesus himself.

This is a truth that dominates the rest of the New Testament: the church is the body of Christ. Paul's letters meditate on this truth at length, drawing out a number of implications. Here we'll mention five:

- If Jesus is the 'head', He goes first. He is the pioneer. As he went through death and into glory, so he will bring us along the same trajectory.

- If we are united to the 'head', then we really are one with him. In fact we are so close that we are 'in Christ', a phrase Paul uses over a hundred times.

- If we are 'in Christ' then what is true of Jesus becomes true for believers too. He is the Son of God; we become children in him. He is the Righteous One; we become righteous in him. He is Abraham's Offspring; we become Abraham's offspring in him—spiritual Israelites and heirs to all the promises of the Old Testament.

- If we are the 'body of Christ' then each believer is a 'member' in that body. We are not all the same. Just as hands, legs and feet are different yet united members of the body, Christians are called to be different yet united members of the church. We belong to each other and use our different giftings to serve each other in love.

And finally...

- If our union with Christ means union with his body, then solo-Christianity cannot exist. A member of Christ needs to be a member of the church.

This last point is why Paul's labours were aimed, almost exclusively, at establishing churches and his writings were intended, almost exclusively, to encourage churches. True Christianity does not produce individual believers so much as a faith-filled *body* that represents Christ to the world.

This world-wide dimension is the fourth lesson which the Damascus Road teaches.

## THE MISSION IS GLOBAL

One of the first things to flow from the Damascus Road was a change of name (Acts 13:9). 'Saul' (his Hebrew name) became 'Paul' (the Greek form of Saul). This change to Greek was significant. In the first century, Greek had a role similar to English in the twenty-first century. It was the language of global communication. If you wanted to remain with your Jewish compatriots, you spoke Hebrew. If you wanted to cross borders and reach the world, you spoke Greek. The Damascus Road produces a 'Paul'—someone who would no longer be a Jew for Jews. Instead he would herald the Jewish Messiah as a light for the nations—

Paul would become a preacher to the 'Gentiles' (that is, the non-Jews).

As Paul preached to non-Jews, a number of questions became pressing: How do we take the ancient Way of Abraham and apply it to believers from wildly different backgrounds? How do we apply the Old Testament to today when Christ has fulfilled the old laws and rituals? How do we govern this spiritual Israel called 'church' now that it is an international movement?

The flashpoints for these issues were controversies about food, clothing and circumcision, but Paul frames and answers these questions as matters of gospel faith. '*Christ* is your life', he writes in Colossians 3—not your nationality, not your tribe, not your diet or your customs or your social standing or your moral performance. All of those claims to identity are boasts in 'the flesh'. Christians live by the Spirit and the Spirit sweeps us up into Christ, to enjoy *his* identity. We are dead to the old boasts of the flesh. In Christ 'there is no [Gentile] or Jew, circumcised or uncircumcised, barbarian, Scythian, slave or free, but Christ is all, and is in all' (Col. 3:11).

If you want to know why Christianity is the largest, most diverse, sociological phenomenon in history, read Paul's letters. As you do, you can be grateful to God for the Damascus Road. It turned a violent xenophobe into a global preacher of peace and unity.

## HAVE YOU SEEN THE LIGHT?

In one sense, none of us can have a Damascus Road experience like Paul's. That was a one-off event in the Bible's story to create a unique figure in the history of God's people. In another sense, though, all of us, whether dramatically or quietly, need the same encounter. We too must know that Jesus is Lord. We too need to know his gracious salvation. We too must become united to him as members of his body. We too must be caught up in his global concern for the nations. However it happens—and reading Paul's writings might be the very best way—we all need to see the light.

*Keep reading…*

### Acts 2
### Acts 26
### Philippians 3

*Keep thinking…*

What were the various truths that the Damascus Road revealed to Paul? How did they impact him?

How have those same truths impacted you, if at all?

If you have read any of Paul's letters, what has struck you most about them?

# 12
# Hallelujah

How do you feel about happy endings? Cynics tend to roll their eyes. *Life doesn't work like that*, they say, trying to look all grown up and sophisticated. *Happy endings are for fairy tales*, they insist, *not real life.*

If we think like this about 'the end', maybe it's because we have bleak thoughts about 'the beginning'. In our opening chapter we thought of four candidates for this world's origin. Each of those beginnings implies a certain ending:

- If we have come from *nothing* then we can only expect to slide back into non-existence.

- If we have come from *chaos* then it seems vain to hope in cosmic harmony.

- If we have come from *power*, then at best we can look forward to slavery.

- But if we have come from *love* then, at last, we have reason to expect a happily ever after.

The Bible's beginning should make us optimists in the end. And indeed the Bible's ending is happy. In fact, of all the world's religious texts, the Bible is the only one that offers hope for these bodies and this world. Other religions may speak of an other-worldly paradise, but they don't speak of the renewal of *this* creation. Only the Bible speaks of such an earthed and earthy future. And no wonder. Only the Bible speaks of the world *loved* into existence. Therefore it's no surprise that the story which begins with family love, ends in feasting joy. The Bible's finale—the book of Revelation—concludes our 'long story' with a dazzling hope.

## REVELATION

After the thirteen letters of Paul, the New Testament continues with eight other letters from various authors (Hebrews to Jude). Some letters were addressed to churches, others to individuals. All concern Christ and how his people should live awaiting his return. Finally, we come to Revelation.

This book can be difficult for a modern reader to understand for many reasons. One significant factor is that it's written in a style that has been dead for two millennia. 'Apocalyptic' literature was very popular in the first century but it's virtually unheard of today. Such writing deals in grand visions as it seeks to unveil the life of heaven.

The 'revelation' spoken of in the book's title consists of the visions given to John, the book's author. John is languishing on a penal colony on account of his faith

(Rev. 1:9), but what does he need? What do any of us need in suffering? A 'revelation' of Jesus.

In chapter 1 John sees Jesus, then in chapters 2–3 Jesus dictates letters to seven churches in Asia Minor (seven is a very prominent number in the book). After this John is given a vision of heaven in which Jesus is depicted as a slain Lamb who is now enthroned (chapters 4–5). From the enthronement of Jesus, the Lamb, we then read seven scenes of judgement that flow from the throne (chapters 6–20).

Other readings of Revelation are available but, if you ask me, these seven scenes are seven angles on the same time period—seven action replays of the history of the world between Christ's first and second coming. In each of these scenes the life of heaven meets the mess and sin of earth. In the end, the Lamb returns to earth, bringing heaven with him and establishing his reign of peace forever (chapters 21–22).

That's the bird's eye view of Revelation but perhaps you have tried to dive down into the details and have got lost. The way John writes can feel alien to us, but stick with it. These things are meant to be understood, and can be. Essentially John's aim is to portray Christ using layer upon layer of images from the rest of Scripture. Coming at the end of the Bible, Revelation is like a collage of all the Scriptures that have come before it. John cuts and pastes biblical motifs— a phrase from the Psalms, an event from the Gospels, a promise from Genesis, an element from the tabernacle, an image from the prophets—and makes of them a bold, technicolour mosaic.

So, to take an example from chapter 19, which we're about to study: Jesus is described as—get this—a Lamb... with blazing eyes... on his wedding day... riding a white horse. The Lamb has multiple crowns on his head... and a sword coming out of his mouth. And this sword is big enough to strike down nations.

This can feel like John is speaking a different language. What are we meant to do with such a description? If we were to draw this scene we would end up laughing at the absurdity of it. But if we let each aspect of the vision resonate in its own way, we'll start to get the picture.

With our Bibles open and with a conviction that the other sixty-five books can help us, we begin to appreciate the multi-faceted wonder of Jesus. We start to realise that John is not being *bizarre*; he's being biblical. A crowned Lamb on horseback makes for an absurd cartoon, but when you understand the symbolism, it makes for heart-warming truth. It means that Jesus, the great Sacrifice (the Lamb), is truly our King (crowned) and riding on the horse tells us that he is extending his reign of peace. How does he rule? Well, the sword coming out of his mouth tells us that he expands his kingdom not by warfare but by what comes out of his mouth. It's the word of Christ that will bring peace to the ends of the earth.

Makes sense, doesn't it? It's just that my 'translation' of the meaning leaves us a little cold. When John says it, using his apocalyptic language, we're left with a proper awe for these realities. That's why I urge you to pick up the book and dive in. Read it for yourself. It won't take you long before you too can speak Revelation.

Here we'll zoom in on chapter 19—one of the book's many angles on the end of the world.

## HAPPY ENDING

In novels, films and fairy tales, happy endings tend to share similar elements. Let me highlight four: the good guys win; the bad guys get their just deserts; there's a wedding; and you finish on a song. Any one of those elements can make us punch the air in glee. In Revelation 19 we see all four in technicolour.

### The Good Guys Win

In verse 6 we read the inspiration for Handel's *Hallelujah Chorus*:

Hallelujah! For our Lord God Almighty reigns.

Perhaps you are remembering it in an older translation. Here's how it appears in Handel's *Messiah*.

Alleluia, Alleluia, Alleluia, Alleluia, Alleluia,
for the Lord God Omnipotent reigneth.

This song of joy celebrates the day when God will be the only power reigning in the world. No more evil, death, curse, sickness or sin. No more threat of nothingness, of chaos, of dark powers. Instead love will reign. The Lord God Almighty will rule in unopposed glory.

When you thought of 'the good guys', who did you think of? The Bible insists that the future belongs to the Almighty Father, ruling through Christ, the Lamb, by the power of his Spirit. They are the 'good guys'. In fact, they are the only 'good guys'. Everyone else is either with them or against them. But the future belongs to God.

### The Bad Guys Get Their Just Deserts

God's justice will be a key part of these future celebrations. According to verse 2, we will sing:

> True and just are his judgments.

And God's judgements will burn against the devil and his servants:

> [They] were thrown alive into the fiery lake of burning sulphur. (Rev. 19:20)

In the old translations, they used the words 'fire and brimstone'. You may have heard of 'fire and brimstone' preaching. Many people today fear 'fire and brimstone' *preaching*. It seems that fewer people fear the 'fire and brimstone' itself.

Yet the Bible insists there is an eternal judgement for the devil *and for all who follow him*. The Bible does not conceal this; it celebrates it.

In fairy tales and films we cheer when the wicked get their come-uppance. In the same way, the Bible says that when Jesus returns his people will cheer as Satan and his followers are judged.

But notice this: in an ultimate sense, the human race isn't either the good guys or the bad guys. We stand between God and the devil and we need to make sure we are found on the right side. How do we ensure that we belong with the good guys?

That's what the next element answers...

## The Wedding

> Let us rejoice and be glad and give him glory! For the wedding of the Lamb has come, and his bride has made herself ready. Fine linen,[1] bright and clean, was given her to wear. (Rev. 19:7-8)

Have you ever wondered why so many happy endings include a wedding? Every one of Shakespeare's comedies finishes with a marriage, sometimes with multiple marriages. Why are our stories about the guy and the girl finally getting together? The Bible says that all of history is headed towards a wedding. Our future hope is a cosmic marriage feast where we celebrate the union of Jesus and his people.

In the verses above, Jesus is described as 'the Lamb' because he is the great Sacrifice who died for our sins. On the other hand, his people are called 'his bride' because they are united to him as in a marriage. This is the key to whether we end up with God or not: are we united to Jesus?

In a marriage you pledge to be one with your spouse. You share a common name, a common home, common money (or common debts!), common possessions. In short, you share a common life. In

---

1. Fine linen stands for the righteous acts of God's holy people.

Revelation 19 we're being told that Jesus wants to share everything with us and if we say 'I will', we share everything with him. Such oneness means that he takes all our debts—our sins—and pays for them on the cross. This is *why* Jesus died as our Lamb. He died because he loves us too much to watch us sink in our own debts. On the cross he says, 'Let your debts be mine, let your darkness be mine, let your death be mine. I will pay.'

Three days later Jesus rose from the dead to say to us, 'I have taken your debts, have my riches. I have taken your death, have my life.' This is beautifully pictured in the verses above: 'fine linen, bright and clean' is *given* to the bride. Jesus provides us with a beautiful covering, all as a sheer gift.

None of us deserve to wear white. We are naturally unclean through our sin. But on the ultimate wedding day and in the presence of God, Christ's people will wear dazzling white. Those who say 'I will' to Jesus instantly receive his righteous covering. He takes our filth and gives us his purity. For free and forever.

This is the good news. The Handsome Prince marries the girl in the gutter and instantly she goes from rags to riches.

This is how we can have our own happy ending. It's how we cross over from the 'bad guys' to the 'good guys'. We cannot buy our way into this Family. No amount of good deeds will earn such a future. But anyone who says 'I will' to Jesus marries into the ultimate Royal Family. They cross over from rags to riches, from the bad guys to the good guys and from a tragic ending to an eternal inheritance.

Which leaves only one response...

## Singing

Four times in this chapter the people cry out in a loud voice, 'Hallelujah!' It's a Hebrew word that means 'Praise the LORD'. And this is what we are built for—celebration, singing, praise.

When an artist has delivered a spine-tingling performance, when your team lifts the trophy, when the concert of a lifetime concludes on a rousing crescendo, we rise to our feet and pour forth praise. It's ecstatic, and it's where creation is headed. Under God, this world is straining ahead on tip-toes towards the Hallelujah Chorus.

When Jesus returns, his people will shout for joy because on that day the good guys win, the bad guys get their come-uppance and we celebrate the ultimate wedding. We won't just sing. We won't be able to stop ourselves singing.

*Keep reading…*

> Revelation 4:1–5:13
> Revelation 19:1-21
> Revelation 21:1–22:21

*Keep thinking…*

How do beliefs about the future affect how we live today?

Where do you think this world is heading? Where do you think you are heading?

What do you think is the right response to Revelation? What is the right response to the Bible?

# Epilogue: And You?

We've come to the story's conclusion. We've seen that it ends well—for creation more generally, for 'the good guys' most specifically, but what about for you personally? That's a question that the Bible should raise for us. How are we ourselves responding? The Bible wasn't written merely to inform us but to involve and to invite us.

There is a 'family' of love and the Son of God welcomes us in. There is a feast of eternal joy and Jesus urges us to join. Are we allowing ourselves to be drawn into the heart of this story? All sixty-six books were written to that end. The very last chapter puts it like this:

> The Spirit and the bride say, 'Come!' And let him who hears say, 'Come!' Whoever is thirsty, let him come; and whoever wishes, let him take the free gift of the water of life. (Rev. 22:17)

The Bible is an invitation. It's an invitation to thirsty people who don't have life and who will perish without Jesus. It's an invitation nonetheless to be one with the Son of God and to feast with him forever. Perhaps you have read these brief chapters and felt your lack, seen Jesus' fullness and heard his call. You may have been a Christian for many years or you may never have considered these things before. Either way, I want to suggest a response you could make. Below are the kind of words you could pray to say 'Yes' to the invitation of the Scriptures:

*Dear Father,*

*Thank you for inviting me into your family. I know I don't deserve it, but thank you for your Son, Jesus, who died for all my sins and rose to give me new life. I turn from the emptiness of living for myself and instead come home to your love and leading. May I know you as Father, may I be one with your Son, may I be filled by your Spirit, now and forever.*

*Amen.*

If you have not felt able to pray a prayer like this, thank you so much for sticking with us to the end of the book. I'd recommend getting into the Bible for yourself; perhaps use the 'Keep Reading' suggestions at the end of each chapter. Or just dive into John's Gospel and pray that God would show you his love in the face of Jesus.

If you have been a Christian for a while, thank you also for reading. I hope you have been refreshed by hearing the big story again and seeing Jesus at the centre. It really is all about him.

If you have prayed a prayer like this for the first time, please tell someone who can help you take your first steps in the Christian life. Christian faith is personal, but it's not private. We live it out in community with others. So get connected to a local church where the Bible is valued and Jesus is loved. Start talking to God in prayer—he loves to hear from you. And keep reading the Scriptures for yourself, because that's where we meet with Jesus—from the beginning to the end.

*Also available from Christian Focus Publications...*

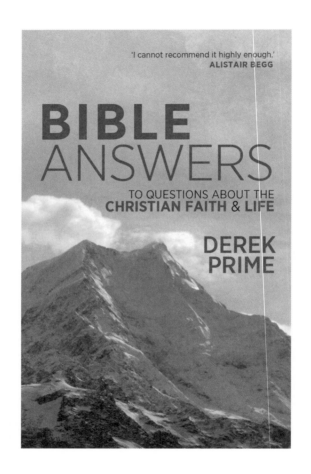

'I cannot recommend it highly enough.'
ALISTAIR BEGG

# BIBLE
# ANSWERS

## TO QUESTIONS ABOUT THE
## CHRISTIAN FAITH & LIFE

## DEREK
## PRIME

978-1-8579-2934-8

# Bible Answers

## To Questions About the Christian Faith & Life

## DEREK PRIME

Many people want to know what the Bible has to say about God and other pressing issues. To meet that need Derek Prime has provided a helpful guide that anyone can use. If you have ever wondered what the Bible really says about something, then this handy guide is where to look.

*Derek Prime addresses crucial questions concisely, practically and, most of all, biblically. This is one of the best books to help us ground our faith in the solid truths of God's Word.*

John Benton
Managing Editor, Evangelicals Now

*It is suitable for young and old, for those newly come to the faith and the experienced believer. Preachers will find it invaluable. Very highly recommended.*

Grace Magazine

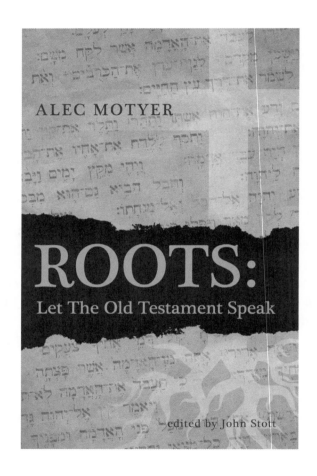

ALEC MOTYER

# ROOTS:
## Let The Old Testament Speak

edited by John Stott

978-1-8455-0506-6

# Roots

## Let the Old Testament Speak

## ALEC MOTYER

The title, Old Testament, creates difficulties of its own. If it is 'Old' and we are people of the 'New', surely we may properly let it fade away into history? Besides, it seems very unlike the New Testament, even contradictory: all those wars when Jesus is the Prince of peace; all those commandments to obey when we are not under law but under grace. And can the God of the Old Testament be a God of love like the Father, Son and Holy Spirit?

These are the questions that Alec Motyer, a lifelong lover of the Old Testament, seeks to answer starting with the conviction that Jesus is the fulfilment of the Old Testament Scripture. This is for the Christian who wants to know what the Old Testament has to do with the New Testament and why the Christian should read it.

*This is vintage Motyer; it is affectionate—the writer's sheer delight in 'the law of the Lord' tends to ooze out from behind the print; it is fresh—he's familiar with the scholarly waterfront but Jacob-like has wrestled and stewed over these texts himself (and his struggle is our gain); it is devious, for Alec clearly wants to hook you on the Old Testament! Huge kudos to Christian Focus for this format.*

Dale Ralph Davis
Minister in Residence, First Presbyterian Church,
Columbia, South Carolina

# GOD'S TIMELINE

## THE BIG BOOK OF CHURCH HISTORY

INCLUDES
16 TIMELINES
& A PULL-OUT
TIMELINE
POSTER

LINDA FINLAYSON

EARLY CHURCH    MEDIEVAL CHURCH    REFORMING CHURCH    MISSIONARY CHURCH    MODERN CHURCH

978-1-5271-0098-5

# God's Timeline

## The Big Book of Church History

### LINDA FINLAYSON

With colour illustrations, pictures, and pull-out timelines, this history book brings the church throughout the ages to life! Learn about the Early, Medieval and Missionary church, passing through key events such as the Council of Nicea and the Reformation—right through to the present day. Find out about the people God used and the impact they had on those around them—including us today!

*This is a helpful and entertaining introduction to the grand sweep of church history. Not only does the text offer a fine narrative of major events and characters but the timeline is especially helpful in allowing children to visualize the interconnection of the events described. A lovely book that will be of help to Sunday school teachers and parents alike.*

Carl R. Trueman
Paul Woolley Professor of Historical Theology and
Church History, Westminster Theological Seminary,
Philadelphia, Pennsylvania

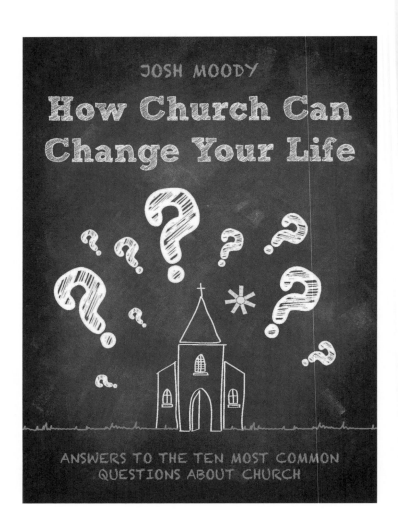

JOSH MOODY

# How Church Can Change Your Life

### ANSWERS TO THE TEN MOST COMMON QUESTIONS ABOUT CHURCH

978-1-7819-1611-7

# How Church Can Change Your Life

Answers to the Ten Most Common Questions about Church

## JOSH MOODY

Google books on church, there will be no shortage of choice! Some will be helpful, others less so. So why another book on church? Josh Moody, is, in fact, asking a very different question: why should I go to church at all? Filled with practical advice, this book will help you answer questions you maybe should have known the answer to and other questions you never knew to ask!

*... a powerful and needed reminder of the central role the local church should play in the life of every Christian.*

R. Albert Mohler
President, The Southern Baptist Theological Seminary,
Louisville, Kentucky

*... a book of great worth. It would make a helpful 'book of the month' on church bookstalls for church members to read and be reminded of what church is meant to be about, or to help non-Christians make progress as they consider the Christian faith.*

Evangelicals Now

# Christian Focus Publications

Our mission statement –

STAYING FAITHFUL

In dependence upon God we seek to impact the world through literature faithful to His infallible Word, the Bible. Our aim is to ensure that the Lord Jesus Christ is presented as the only hope to obtain forgiveness of sin, live a useful life and look forward to heaven with Him.

Our books are published in four imprints:

### CHRISTIAN
## FOCUS

Popular works including biographies, commentaries, basic doctrine and Christian living.

### CHRISTIAN
## HERITAGE

Books representing some of the best material from the rich heritage of the church.

## MENTOR

Books written at a level suitable for Bible College and seminary students, pastors, and other serious readers. The imprint includes commentaries, doctrinal studies, examination of current issues and church history.

## CF4•K

Children's books for quality Bible teaching and for all age groups: Sunday school curriculum, puzzle and activity books; personal and family devotional titles, biographies and inspirational stories – because you are never too young to know Jesus!

Christian Focus Publications Ltd,
Geanies House, Fearn, Ross-shire,
IV20 1TW, Scotland, United Kingdom.
www.christianfocus.com
blog.christianfocus.com